BIG IDEAS
MATH.
GREEN

Record and Practice Journal

- Activity Recording Journal

- Activity Manipulatives

- Extra Practice Worksheets

- Fair Game Review Worksheets

- Glossary

BIG IDEAS
LEARNING.

Erie, Pennsylvania

ISBN 13: 978-1-60840-232-8
ISBN 10: 1-60840-232-0

23456789-VLP-15 14 13 12 11

Contents

Contents

Contents

Contents

Contents

Contents

Additional Topics

Name_____ Date_____

Fair Game Review

Find the area.

1.

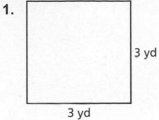

3 yd

3 yd

2.

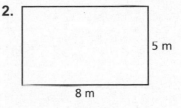

5 m

8 m

3.

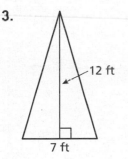

12 ft

7 ft

4.

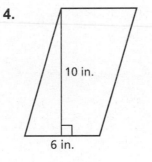

10 in.

6 in.

5.

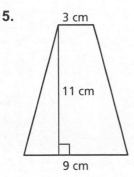

3 cm

11 cm

9 cm

6.

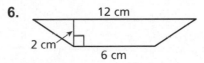

12 cm

2 cm

6 cm

7. An office building has a window shaped like a parallelogram. The window has a base that is 12 inches and a height that is 10 inches. What is the area of the window?

Chapter 1 **Fair Game Review** (continued)

Simplify the expression.

8. $9 - 6 \div 3$

9. $4 \bullet 8 - 2 \div 2$

10. $8 + (10 - 4)$

11. $6^2 - 7(2)$

12. $3 \bullet 7 \bullet 2$

13. $(5^2 + 1) \div 13$

14. $40 - 5 \bullet 7 + 11$

15. $10 - (2 + 1)^2$

16. You and three friends go to a restaurant for dinner. You buy three appetizers that cost $6 each. You also buy two desserts that cost $3 each. You split the total bill evenly. How much do you pay?

1.1 Evaluating Algebraic Expressions
For use with Activity 1.1

Essential Question How can you write and evaluate an expression that represents a real-life problem?

1 EXAMPLE: Reading and Re-Reading

> You are babysitting for 3 hours. You will receive $12.
> What is your hourly wage?

- Underline the numbers and units you need to solve the problem.

- Read the problem carefully a second time. Underline the key word for the question in another color.

- Write each important number and word, with its units, on a small piece of paper. Make five other pieces of paper with +, −, ×, ÷, and =.

- Arrange the pieces of paper to form an equation. Use it to answer the key word question "What is your hourly wage?" Make sure the units for the key word are the same as the units in the expression.

- Evaluate the expression on the right side of the equation.

Your hourly wage is _____.

1.1 **Evaluating Algebraic Expressions** (continued)

2 **ACTIVITY:** Reading and Re-Reading

Work with a partner. Use the strategy shown in Example 1 to write an expression for each problem. After you have written the expression, evaluate it using mental math or some other method.

a. You are washing cars for 2 hours. You will receive $6. How much will you earn per hour?

Expression: Expression: _____

Amount you earn per hour: _____

b. You have $60. You buy a pair of jeans and a shirt. The pair of jeans costs $27. You come home with $15. How much did you spend on the shirt?

Expression: _____

Amount you spend on shirt: _____

c. For lunch, you buy 5 sandwiches that cost $3 each. How much do you spend?

Expression: _____

Amount you spend on sandwiches: _____

1.1 **Evaluating Algebraic Expressions** (continued)

d. You are running a 4500-foot race. How much farther do you have left to go after running 2000 feet?

Expression: _____

Amount left to go: _____

e. A young rattlesnake grows at a rate of about 20 centimeters per year. How much does a young rattlesnake grow in 2 years?

Expression: _____

Amount rattlesnake grows in 2 years: _____

What Is Your Answer?

3. IN YOUR OWN WORDS How can you write and evaluate an expression that represents a real-life problem? Give one example with addition, one with subtraction, one with multiplication, and one with division.

Name _____ Date _____

1.1 Practice
For use after Lesson 1.1

Evaluate the expression when $a = 4$, $b = 5$, and $c = 10$.

1. $a + 7$

2. $b - 3$

3. $9c$

4. $25 \div b$

5. $a \bullet c$

6. $b - a$

7. $a + b + c$

8. $\dfrac{c}{b}$

9. $4a - 7$

10. $b^2 + 2.5$

11. $\dfrac{c}{5} + 6a$

12. $bc - 13$

13. After m minutes, an adult blinks about $10m + 3$ times. About how many times does an adult blink in three minutes? in two hours?

14. You need $2b$ cups of flour for making b loaves of bread. You have 8 cups of flour. Do you have enough for 5 loaves of bread? Explain.

15. The expression $9a + 6s$ is the cost for a adults and s students to see a musical performance.

    a. Find the total cost for three adults and five students.

    b. The number of adults and students in a group both double. Does the cost double? Explain your answer using an example.

    c. The number of students doubles, but the number of adults is cut in half. Is the cost the same? Explain your answer using an example.

Name_____ Date _____

 1.2 **Writing Expressions**
For use with Activity 1.2

Essential Question Which words correspond to the four operations of
addition, subtraction, multiplication, and division?

1 **ACTIVITY:** Words That Imply Addition or Subtraction

Work with a partner.

a. Complete the table.

Variable	Phrase	Expression
n	4 more than a number	$n + 4$ or $4 + n$
m	The difference of a number and 3	$m - 3$
x	The sum of a number and 8	
p	10 less than a number	
n	7 units farther away	$n + 7$ or $7 + n$
t	8 minutes sooner	
w	12 minutes later	
y	A number increased by 9	

Here is a word problem that uses one of the expressions in the table.

You arrive at the pizza shop 8 minutes sooner than your friend.
Your friend arrives at 6:42 P.M. When did you arrive?

b. Which expression from the table can you use to solve the
problem?

c. Write a problem that uses a different expression from the table.

.2 **Writing Expressions** (continued)

2 **ACTIVITY:** Words That Imply Multiplication or Division

Work with a partner. Match each phrase with an expression.

The product of a number and 3	$n \div 3$
The quotient of 3 and a number	$4p$
4 times a number	$n \bullet 3$
A number divided by 3	$2m$
Twice a number	$3 \div n$

ACTIVITY: Find the Intruder

Work with a partner.

A ship can pass through a gate only if the gate expression can be found in its ID number.

For instance, the ID number JK – 5 + NM contains the expression K – 5. So the ship is allowed through the gate marked "5 less than a number."

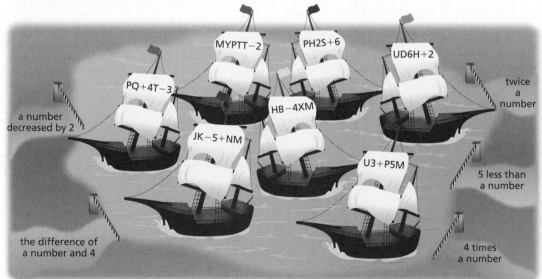

a. Circle the ships that are allowed in the lake. Put an X through the ships that are intruders.

1.2 **Writing Expressions** (continued)

b. Make up your own "Find the Intruder" game. Describe your game in the space provided. Trade games with your partner. Solve the game and talk about your solution.

What Is Your Answer?

4. Which words correspond to each operation? In each box, write any words that imply the operation.

+	−	×	÷

5. Write a phrase for each expression.

a. $n + 6$

b. $4 - x$

c. $3x + 1$

d. $2x$

Name_____ Date _____

 1.2 **Practice**
For use after Lesson 1.2

Write the phrase as an expression.

1. the total of 8 and 13

2. 42 divided by 7

3. a number a multiplied by 12

4. the difference of a number b and 10

Give two ways to write the expression as a phrase.

5. $6 + p$

6. $9m$

Write the phrase as an expression. Then evaluate when $x = 3$ and $y = 15$.

7. 7 more than the quotient of a number y and 5

8. twice the sum of a number x and 8

9. An ice skater is penalized 1.2 points for a fall. Write an expression for the ice skater's final score.

10. You earn $7 for every hour that you babysit.

  a. Complete the table.

Hours	1	2	3	4	5	6	7	8
Earnings								

  b. Write an expression for the amount you earn after h hours.

  c. How much will you earn after babysitting for 12 hours? Explain your reasoning.

1.3 Properties of Addition and Multiplication
For use with Activity 1.3

Essential Question Does the order in which you perform an operation matter?

1 ACTIVITY: Does Order Matter?

Work with a partner. Place each statement in the correct oval.

a. Fasten 5 shirt buttons.

b. Put on a shirt and tie.

c. Fill and seal an envelope.

d. Floss your teeth.

e. Put on your shoes.

f. Chew and swallow.

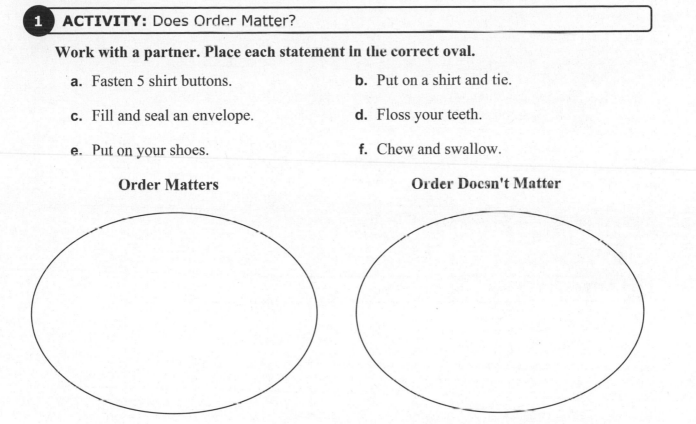

Order Matters

Order Doesn't Matter

Write some math problems using the four operations where order matters and some where order doesn't matter.

1.3 **Properties of Addition and Multiplication** (continued)

2 **ACTIVITY:** Commutative Properties

Work with a partner.

   a. Circle the statements that are true.

   $3 + 5 \overset{?}{=} 5 + 3$ $3 - 5 \overset{?}{=} 5 - 3$

   $9 \times 3 \overset{?}{=} 3 \times 9$ $9 \div 3 \overset{?}{=} 3 \div 9$

   b. The true equations show the Commutative Properties of Addition and Multiplication. Why are they called "commutative?" Write the properties.

3 **ACTIVITY:** Associative Properties

Work with a partner.

   a. Circle the statements that are true.

   $8 + (3 + 1) \overset{?}{=} (8 + 3) + 1$ $8 - (3 - 1) \overset{?}{=} (8 - 3) - 1$

   $12 \times (6 \times 2) \overset{?}{=} (12 \times 6) \times 2$ $12 \div (6 \div 2) \overset{?}{=} (12 \div 6) \div 2$

   b. The true equations show the Associative Properties of Addition and Multiplication. Why are they called "associative?" Write the properties.

What Is Your Answer?

   4. IN YOUR OWN WORDS Does the order in which you perform an operation matter?

1.3   Properties of Addition and Multiplication (continued)

5. MENTAL MATH Explain how you can use the Commutative and Associative Properties of Addition to add the sum in your head.

$$11 + 7 + 12 + 13 + 8 + 9$$

6. SECRET CODE The creatures on a distant planet use the symbols ■, ◆, ★, and ● for the four operations.

    a. Use the codes to decide which symbol represents addition and which symbol represents multiplication. Explain your reasoning.

$$3 \bullet 4 = 4 \bullet 3$$

$$3 \bigstar 4 = 4 \bigstar 3$$

$$2 \bullet (5 \bullet 3) = (2 \bullet 5) \bullet 3$$

$$2 \bigstar (5 \bigstar 3) = (2 \bigstar 5) \bigstar 3$$

$$0 \bullet 4 = 0$$

$$0 \bigstar 4 = 4$$

    b. Make up your own symbols for addition and multiplication. Write codes using your symbols. Trade codes with a classmate. Decide which symbol represents addition and which symbol represents multiplication.

1.3 Practice
For use after Lesson 1.3

Tell which property is illustrated by the statement.

1. $x \cdot 1 = x$

2. $4.8 + k = k + 4.8$

Simplify the expression. Explain each step.

3. $8 + (7 + x)$

4. $10(11a)$

5. $0 \cdot v \cdot 12$

Complete the statement using the specified property.

	Property	Statement
6.	Addition Property of Zero	$(b + 0) + 6 =$
7.	Commutative Property of Multiplication	$3 \cdot (n \cdot 5) =$

8. The expression $10 \cdot x \cdot 15$ represents the volume of a swimming pool. Simplify the expression.

9. You earn 10 points for every coin you collect in a video game. Then you find a star that triples your score.

   a. Write an expression for the number of points you earn from the coins.

   b. Write and simplify an expression for the total number of points you earn.

Name_____ Date _____

1.4 The Distributive Property
For use with Activity 1.4

Essential Question How do you multiply two 2-digit numbers using mental math?

1 ACTIVITY: Finding Products Involving Multiples of 10

Working with a partner, take turns using mental math to find the product.

Read the expression to your partner. Then ask your partner to write the answer. Switch roles and repeat until you have each read four expressions.

    a. 10×20 **b.** 10×30 **c.** 10×13 **d.** 24×10

    e. 20×25 **f.** 30×12 **g.** 13×40 **h.** 30×70

In Activity 1, you used mental math to find simple products. You can use the *Distributive Property* and mental math to find more complicated products.

2 ACTIVITY: Using Mental Math

Work with a partner. Use the Distributive Property and mental math to find the product.

    a. 6×23

    b. 4×17

    c. 8×26

    d. 7×33

    e. 9×47

1.4 **The Distributive Property** (continued)

3 **ACTIVITY:** Two Ways to Multiply

Work with a partner. Find the product two different ways. Compare the two methods.

a. 63×28

Method 1	**Method 2**
63	63
$\times 28$	$\times 28$

b. 32×45 **c.** 37×61

d. 28×57 **e.** 17×43

1.4 The Distributive Property (continued)

4 ACTIVITY: Using Mental Math

Work with a partner. Use the Distributive Property and mental math to find the product.

  a. 60×49

  b. 20×19

  c. 40×29

  d. 25×39

  e. 15×47

What Is Your Answer?

5. **IN YOUR OWN WORDS** How can you multiply two 2-digit numbers using mental math? Use an example in your answer.

Name _____ Date _____

1.4 Practice
For use after Lesson 1.4

Use the Distributive Property and mental math to find the product.

1. 4×31

2. 7×49

3. 13×102

4. $6(19)$

5. $23(42)$

6. $16(38)$

Use the Distributive Property to simplify the expression.

7. $8(5 + w)$

8. $11(9 + d)$

9. $15(p - 4)$

10. $4(21 - n)$

11. $20(y + 10)$

12. $9(12 - k)$

13. A practice field is 75 yards long and 29 yards wide. Use the Distributive Property and mental math to find the area of the practice field.

14. You have a rectangular fort that is 7 feet long and 6 feet wide. You decide to add x feet to the length of the fort.

   a. Find the area of the fort before the addition.

   b. Use the Distributive Property to write and simplify an expression for the area of the fort with the addition.

   c. You have 90 square feet of space available for your fort. What is the maximum value of x feet that you can add to the length?

Name_____ Date_____

Essential Question How can you use formulas to find the area of an object with an unusual shape?

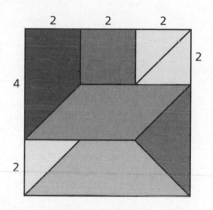

---

1 **ACTIVITY:** Using an Area Formula

Work with a partner. Complete the table.

Polygon	Name	Area Formula	Area
square (sides s, s)			
trapezoid (b, h, B)			
parallelogram (h, b)			
triangle (h, b)			
trapezoid (b, h, B)			
right triangle (h, b)			

1.5 **Using Formulas to Solve Problems** (continued)

2 **ACTIVITY:** Finding an Area

Work with a partner. Use the shapes from Activity 1 to find the area of the sailboat. Explain your reasoning.*

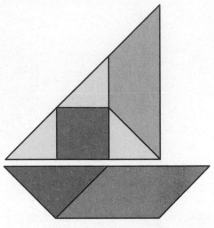

3 **ACTIVITY:** Finding an Area

Work with a partner. Use the shapes from Activity 1 to create the picture. Then draw the outline of each shape on the figure to show how you created the picture.

a. house

20 square units

b. rabbit

36 square units

c. bird

32 square units

*Cut-outs are available in the back of the Record and Practice Journal.

1.5 **Using Formulas to Solve Problems** (continued)

What Is Your Answer?

4. **IN YOUR OWN WORDS** How can you use formulas to find the area of an object with an unusual shape?

5. Show how you can use the formula $A = bh$ for the area of a rectangle to write the formula for the area of a parallelogram.

6. Show how you can use the formula $A = bh$ for the area of a rectangle to write the formula for the area of a triangle.

Name _____ Date _____

Use a formula to find the area of the figure.

1.
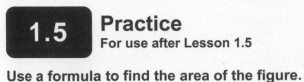
18 in.

22 in.

2.

4 in.

5 in.

3.
6 m

5 m

2 m

4. In football, a player's average number of yards per carry is the average number of yards gained divided by the number of times the player carries the ball. What is the average number of yards per carry for a player who gained 156 yards on 12 carries?

$$\text{Average number of yards per carry} = \frac{\text{Number of yards gained}}{\text{Number of carries}}$$

5. A rectangular lawn is 60 feet wide and 90 feet long.

   a. What is the area of the lawn?

   b. A bag of fertilizer covers 50 square feet. How many bags of fertilizer do you need to cover the entire lawn? Explain.

Fair Game Review

Find the sum or difference.

1. $\dfrac{2}{3} + \dfrac{1}{6}$

2. $\dfrac{5}{8} + \dfrac{7}{12}$

3. $\dfrac{4}{5} + \dfrac{5}{9}$

4. $\dfrac{3}{5} - \dfrac{1}{10}$

5. $\dfrac{9}{14} - \dfrac{4}{7}$

6. $\dfrac{8}{11} - \dfrac{4}{15}$

7. In January, you grew $\dfrac{1}{3}$ of an inch. By the end of the year, you grew $\dfrac{7}{8}$ of an inch. How much did you grow from February to December?

Name _____ Date _____

Write the mixed number as an improper fraction.

8. $2\dfrac{1}{3}$

9. $4\dfrac{3}{5}$

10. $9\dfrac{9}{10}$

11. $5\dfrac{7}{8}$

Write the improper fraction as a mixed number.

12. $\dfrac{12}{7}$

13. $\dfrac{30}{11}$

14. $\dfrac{33}{4}$

15. $\dfrac{83}{20}$

16. A recipe calls for $2\dfrac{3}{4}$ cups of flour. Write the mixed number as an improper fraction. How many one-fourth cups do you need?

2.1 Fractions and Estimation
For use with Activity 2.1

Essential Question How can you use estimation to check that your answer is reasonable?

1 ACTIVITY: Using Models for Fractions

Work with a partner. Use the model for the whole to draw a model for the given fractions.

Whole	Model for the Whole	Fractions	Model for Fraction
a. Sample: Circle	(circle)	$\dfrac{5}{8}$	
b. Circle	(circle)	$\dfrac{3}{4}, \dfrac{5}{12}, \dfrac{4}{6}$	
c. Rectangle	(rectangle)	$\dfrac{3}{5}, \dfrac{4}{5}, \dfrac{7}{10}$	
d. Counters	○ ○ ○ ○ ○ ○ ○ ○	$\dfrac{1}{2}, \dfrac{3}{8}, \dfrac{3}{4}$	
e. Piece of Paper	(square)	$\dfrac{7}{8}, \dfrac{1}{8}, \dfrac{1}{4}$	

2 ACTIVITY: Estimating Sums and Differences

Work with a partner. Add or subtract. Then check your answer by using one of the models in Activity 1 to estimate the sum or difference.

a. $\dfrac{1}{6} + \dfrac{1}{4}$

2.1   **Fractions and Estimation** (continued)

b. $\dfrac{1}{3} + \dfrac{1}{4}$

c. $\dfrac{5}{8} + \dfrac{1}{3}$

d. $\dfrac{7}{8} - \dfrac{1}{3}$

e. $\dfrac{2}{3} - \dfrac{4}{9}$

3   **ACTIVITY: Estimating Products**

Work with a partner. Use a fraction model to choose $0, \dfrac{1}{4}, \dfrac{1}{2}, \dfrac{3}{4}$, or 1 as the best estimate of the product.

a. $\dfrac{2}{3} \times \dfrac{7}{8}$

b. $\dfrac{1}{5} \times \dfrac{3}{10}$

c. $\dfrac{3}{4} \times \dfrac{5}{7}$

d. $\dfrac{7}{8} \times \dfrac{7}{8}$

2.1 Fractions and Estimation (continued)

4 ACTIVITY: Estimating Quotients

Work with a partner. Use a fraction model to choose $0, \frac{1}{4}, \frac{1}{2}, \frac{3}{4}$, or 1 as the best estimate of the quotient.

a. $\frac{5}{9} \div 2$

b. $\frac{3}{5} \div 3$

c. $\frac{1}{2} \div 8$

d. $\frac{5}{6} \div 2$

What Is Your Answer?

5. **IN YOUR OWN WORDS** How can you use estimation to check that your answer is reasonable? Give some examples.

Name _____ Date _____

Practice
For use after Lesson 2.1

Estimate the product or quotient.

1. $\dfrac{3}{4} \times \dfrac{10}{13}$

2. $\dfrac{7}{9} \times \dfrac{3}{7}$

3. $\dfrac{5}{6} \div 2$

4. $\dfrac{17}{20} \div \dfrac{8}{9}$

Use compatible numbers to estimate the product or quotient.

5. $122 \times \dfrac{3}{11}$

6. $81 \times \dfrac{1}{4}$

7. $142 \div 13\dfrac{13}{16}$

8. $20 \div 7\dfrac{1}{5}$

Estimate the value of the expression.

9. $14\dfrac{8}{9} \div 2\dfrac{12}{13} \times 5\dfrac{1}{3}$

10. $3\dfrac{5}{7} \times 8\dfrac{2}{11} \div 1\dfrac{9}{10}$

11. $55\dfrac{11}{14} \div \left(2\dfrac{3}{10} \times 3\dfrac{14}{15}\right)$

12. A cereal box holds $25\dfrac{1}{4}$ ounces of cereal. A serving size is 8 ounces.

   About how many servings are in the box of cereal?

13. Your team runs $2\dfrac{3}{10}$ miles at the beginning of each practice. You have

   5 practices each week. About how many miles do you run in a week?

14. You paint a wall that is $7\dfrac{5}{9}$ feet by $14\dfrac{1}{6}$ feet. A quart of paint covers

   40 square feet. Are 3 quarts of paint enough to paint the wall? Explain.

Name_____ Date_____

2.2 Multiplying Fractions and Whole Numbers
For use with Activity 2.2

Essential Question What does it mean when a whole number is multiplied by a fraction? Will the product be *greater than* or *less than* the whole number?

1 EXAMPLE: Multiplying a Fraction and a Whole Number

You have 3 gallons of paint. You use $\frac{3}{4}$ of the paint. How many gallons did you use?

THINK ABOUT THE QUESTION: One way to think about this question is to rewrite the question.

Words: What is $\frac{3}{4}$ of 3?   **Numbers:** $\frac{3}{4} \times 3 = ?$

Here is one way to get the answer.

- **Draw** a segment to represent a length of 3.

- **Show** how to divide 3 into 4 equal parts.

- **Rewrite** the number 3 as a fraction whose numerator is divisible by 4.

- Each part is $\frac{3}{4}$ gallon and you used three of them. Written as multiplication, you have $\frac{3}{4} \times 3 = $ _____.

- You used _____ gallons of paint.

2.2 **Multiplying Fractions and Whole Numbers** (continued)

2 **EXAMPLE:** Multiplying a Whole Number and a Fraction

Use the number line to find $4 \times \dfrac{2}{5}$. Describe your steps.

$$
\begin{array}{c}
\leftarrow\!\!\!-\!\!+\!\!-\!\!+\!\!-\!\!+\!\!-\!\!+\!\!-\!\!+\!\!-\!\!+\!\!-\!\!+\!\!-\!\!+\!\!-\!\!+\!\!-\!\!+\!\!-\!\!\rightarrow \\
\;0\quad \tfrac{1}{5}\quad \tfrac{2}{5}\quad \tfrac{3}{5}\quad \tfrac{4}{5}\quad 1\quad \tfrac{6}{5}\quad \tfrac{7}{5}\quad \tfrac{8}{5}\quad \tfrac{9}{5}\quad 2
\end{array}
$$

$4 \times \dfrac{2}{5} =$ _____ .

Inductive Reasoning

Work with a partner. Complete the table using a number line.

	Exercise	Repeated Addition
1	**3.** $\dfrac{3}{4} \times 3$	
2	**4.** $4 \times \dfrac{2}{5}$	
	5. $\dfrac{7}{6} \times 5$	
	6. $3 \times \dfrac{9}{5}$	
	7. $\dfrac{1}{3} \times 12$	

2.2 **Multiplying Fractions and Whole Numbers** (continued)

What Is Your Answer?

8. a. Write a real-life problem that is related to the product $\dfrac{2}{3} \times 5$.

  b. Write a different real-life problem that is related to the product $5 \times \dfrac{2}{3}$.

  c. Are the two products equal? How is your answer related to the Commutative Property of Multiplication?

9. IN YOUR OWN WORDS What does it mean when a whole number is multiplied by a fraction? Will the product be *greater than* or *less than* the whole number?

10. Write a general rule for multiplying fractions and whole numbers.

Name _____ Date _____

2.2 Practice
For use after Lesson 2.2

Multiply. Write the answer in simplest form.

1. $4 \times \dfrac{1}{9}$

2. $8 \times \dfrac{2}{5}$

3. $\dfrac{3}{8} \times 9$

4. $\dfrac{11}{2} \times 7$

5. $9 \times \dfrac{7}{9}$

6. $\dfrac{2}{3} \times 12$

Evaluate the expression when $x = 4$, $y = \dfrac{4}{15}$, and $z = 30$.

7. $\dfrac{5}{8} \cdot z$

8. xyz

9. $\dfrac{1}{2} + yz$

10. You design a shirt that requires $\dfrac{5}{6}$ yard of fabric. Four friends ask you to make them a shirt. How many yards of fabric do you need?

11. The table shows the amount of iced tea mix that is needed for each amount of water shown.

Iced tea mix	Water
1-1/2 tbsp	1 cup
2 tbsp	1 quart (4 cups)
1/4 cup	2 quarts (8 cups)
1/2 cup	1 gallon (4 quarts)

   a. Give two possible ways to make 11 cups of iced tea.

   b. How much mix will you need for each of your methods? Explain.

Name_____ Date _____

2.3 Multiplying Fractions
For use with Activity 2.3

Essential Question What does it mean to multiply fractions?

1 **EXAMPLE:** Multiplying Fractions

A bottle of water is $\frac{4}{5}$ full. You drink $\frac{2}{3}$ of the water. How much do you drink?

THINK ABOUT THE QUESTION: To help you think about this question, rewrite the question.

Words: What is $\frac{2}{3}$ of $\frac{4}{5}$? **Numbers:** $\frac{2}{3} \times \frac{4}{5} = ?$

Here is one way to get the answer.

- **Draw** a segment to represent a length of $\frac{4}{5}$.

- **Show** how to divide $\frac{4}{5}$ into three equal parts.

- **Rewrite** $\frac{4}{5}$ as a fraction whose numerator is divisible by 3.

- Each part is $\frac{4}{15}$ of the water and you drank two of them. Written

  as multiplication, you have $\frac{2}{3} \times \frac{4}{5} = $ _____.

You drank _____ of the water.

Name _____ Date _____

2 **EXAMPLE:** Multiplying Fractions

A park has a playground that is $\frac{3}{4}$ of its width and $\frac{4}{5}$ of its length. **What fraction of the park is covered by the playground?**

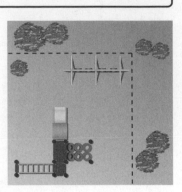

Fold a piece of paper horizontally into fourths and shade three of the fourths to represent $\frac{3}{4}$.

Fold the paper vertically into fifths and shade $\frac{4}{5}$ of the paper another color.

Count the total number of squares. This number is the denominator. The numerator is the number of squares shaded with both colors.

$\frac{3}{4} \times \frac{4}{5} = $ _____ .

Inductive Reasoning

Work with a partner. Complete the table using a model or paper folding.

	Exercise	Verbal Expression	Answer
1	3. $\frac{2}{3} \times \frac{4}{5}$		
2	4. $\frac{3}{4} \times \frac{4}{5}$		
	5. $\frac{2}{3} \times \frac{5}{6}$		
	6. $\frac{1}{6} \times \frac{1}{4}$		
	7. $\frac{2}{5} \times \frac{1}{2}$		
	8. $\frac{5}{8} \times \frac{4}{5}$		

2.3 **Multiplying Fractions** (continued)

What Is Your Answer?

9. **IN YOUR OWN WORDS** What does it mean to multiply fractions?

10. Write a general rule for multiplying fractions.

Name _____ Date _____

Multiply. Write the answer in simplest form.

1. $\dfrac{1}{6} \times \dfrac{5}{8}$

2. $\dfrac{7}{9} \times 3$

3. $\dfrac{8}{9} \times \dfrac{3}{5}$

4. $\dfrac{2}{7} \times \dfrac{7}{4}$

5. $\dfrac{3}{4} \times \dfrac{6}{11} \times \dfrac{3}{2}$

6. $\dfrac{9}{10} \times \dfrac{7}{9} \times \dfrac{5}{8}$

7. $\left(\dfrac{5}{8}\right)^2$

8. $\left(\dfrac{1}{2}\right)^2 \times \left(\dfrac{8}{9}\right)^2$

9. You reserve $\dfrac{2}{5}$ of the seats on a tour bus. You are able to fill $\dfrac{5}{8}$ of the seats you reserve. What fraction of the seats on the bus are you able to fill?

10. You survey 200 people about the electronics they own. The results show that $\dfrac{33}{40}$ people own a cell phone. Of these people, $\dfrac{10}{11}$ also own an MP3 player.

   a. What fraction of the people own a cell phone and an MP3 player?

   b. How many people own a cell phone, but not an MP3 player? Explain.

Name_____ Date_____

Essential Question   How do you multiply a mixed number by a fraction?

1 ACTIVITY: Multiplying a Mixed Number and a Fraction

Work with a partner. Use a diagram to find the product.

a. $1\frac{1}{2} \times \frac{2}{3}$

b. $\frac{4}{9} \times 2\frac{1}{4}$

c. $2\frac{1}{4} \times \frac{1}{2}$

d. $\frac{1}{3} \times 3\frac{3}{4}$

2.4   **Multiplying Mixed Numbers** (continued)

2   **ACTIVITY:** Multiplying a Mixed Number and a Fraction

Work with a partner. How many square feet are in the piece of fabric?

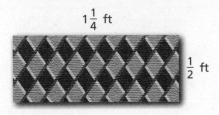

$1\frac{1}{4}$ ft

$\frac{1}{2}$ ft

a. Use the Distributive Property and find the sum of the two pieces.

b. Rewrite the mixed number as an improper fraction and multiply.

3   **ACTIVITY:** Buried Treasure Game

Number of Players: 2

Use the map on the next page. Taking turns, each player will

- choose a treasure location.

- roll a number cube as many times as there are blanks in the expression.

- place the numbers in the blanks to form the greatest possible value for that treasure location.

- check each other's work.

- repeat the steps until all expressions are used.

Players then total the values of their treasures (sum of the three expressions). The player with the greater total wins the game.

2.4 **Multiplying Mixed Numbers** (continued)

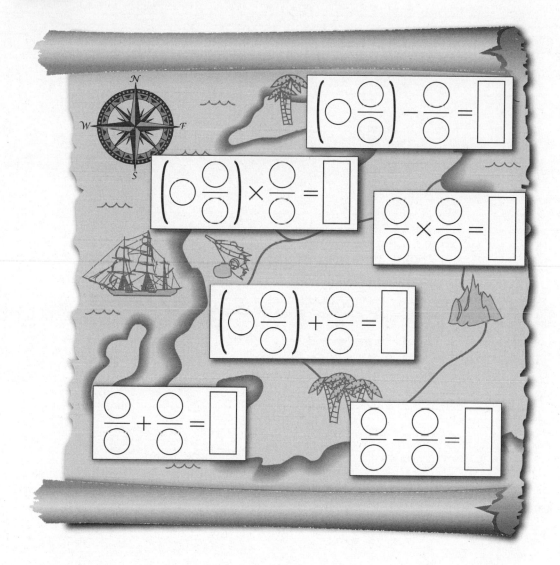

What Is Your Answer?

4. **IN YOUR OWN WORDS** How do you multiply a mixed number by a fraction?

2.4 Practice
For use after Lesson 2.4

Use the Distributive Property to find the product.

1. $\dfrac{5}{6} \times 2\dfrac{2}{5}$

2. $4\dfrac{4}{9} \times \dfrac{1}{10}$

3. $8\dfrac{2}{3} \times \dfrac{3}{4}$

Multiply. Write the answer in simplest form.

4. $\dfrac{7}{8} \times 2\dfrac{1}{3}$

5. $7 \times 3\dfrac{9}{14}$

6. $5\dfrac{5}{9} \times 2\dfrac{7}{10}$

7. $9\dfrac{3}{7} \times \dfrac{5}{11} \times \dfrac{14}{15}$

8. $10\dfrac{5}{12} \times 3\dfrac{3}{25} \times 4$

9. $12\dfrac{1}{4} \times 2\dfrac{2}{21} \times 3\dfrac{3}{4}$

10. You spend $3\dfrac{1}{2}$ hours doing homework. You spend $\dfrac{1}{4}$ of that time doing homework for social studies. How much time do you spend doing social studies homework?

11. A triangle has a base of $5\dfrac{2}{3}$ inches and a height of 3 inches. What is the area of the triangle?

2.5 Dividing Fractions
For use with Activity 2.5

Essential Question How do you divide by a fraction?

1 ACTIVITY: Dividing by a Fraction

Work with a partner.

a. Describe the pattern of the divisors in the first column. (16 is the divisor of $8 \div 16$.)

b. Describe the pattern of the numbers in the second column. Use the pattern to complete the table.

$8 \div 16$	$\frac{1}{2}$
$8 \div 8$	1
$8 \div 4$	2
$8 \div 2$	4
$8 \div 1$	8
$8 \div \frac{1}{2}$	
$8 \div \frac{1}{4}$	
$8 \div \frac{1}{8}$	

c. The division $8 \div \frac{1}{2}$ can be read as "How many halves are in 8?" Use the completed table to answer this question. Then draw a model that shows your answer.

d. Use the pattern in the table to complete the following.

$8 \div \frac{1}{2} = 16 = 8 \times \frac{2}{1}$ Invert $\frac{1}{2}$ and multiply.

$8 \div \frac{1}{4} = 32 = $ [ ] [ ]

$8 \div \frac{1}{8} = 64 = $ [ ] [ ]

2.5 **Dividing Fractions** (continued)

2 **ACTIVITY:** Dividing by a Fraction

Work with a partner.

  a. Draw a model for $3 \div \dfrac{2}{3}$. Use the model to answer the question

   "How many two-thirds are in 3?"

  b. Complete the table in two ways. First use the model. Then use the "invert and multiply" rule that you found in Activity 1. Compare your answers.

$3 \div \dfrac{2}{3}$	
$6 \div \dfrac{2}{3}$	
$9 \div \dfrac{2}{3}$	
$12 \div \dfrac{2}{3}$	

3 **ACTIVITY:** Dividing by a Fraction

Work with a partner. Write the division problem and answer it using a model.

  a. How many halves are in five halves?

  b. How many sixths are in three halves?

2.5 **Dividing Fractions** (continued)

    c. How many three-fourths are in 3?

    d. How many four-fifths are in 8?

    e. How many three-tenths are in 6?

    f. How many halves are in a fourth?

What Is Your Answer?

    4. IN YOUR OWN WORDS How do you divide by a fraction? Give an example.

2.5 Practice
For use after Lesson 2.5

Complete the statement.

1. $\dfrac{3}{8} \times$ _____ $= 1$
2. $7 \times$ _____ $= 1$
3. $3 \div$ _____ $= 36$
4. $\dfrac{4}{9} \div$ _____ $= 12$

Evaluate the expression.

5. $\dfrac{1}{3} \div \dfrac{1}{6}$

6. $\dfrac{3}{8} \div \dfrac{5}{8}$

7. $6 \div \dfrac{2}{5}$

8. $\dfrac{4}{9} \div \dfrac{2}{3} \div \dfrac{5}{6}$

9. $\dfrac{1}{3} + \dfrac{4}{7} \div \dfrac{3}{10}$

10. $\dfrac{7}{8} \bullet \dfrac{4}{5} \div \dfrac{7}{20}$

11. In a jewelry store, rings make up $\dfrac{5}{9}$ of the inventory. Earrings make up $\dfrac{4}{15}$ of the inventory. How many times greater is the ring inventory than the earring inventory?

12. You have $\dfrac{3}{4}$ of a book to read for your book report. You need to finish it in 10 days.

   a. What fraction of the book do you need to read each day?

   b. The book has 120 total pages. How many pages do you need to read each day?

Name_____ Date _____

Essential Question How can you use division by a mixed number as part of a story?

1 EXAMPLE: Writing a Story

Write a story that uses the division problem $6 \div 1\frac{1}{2}$. Draw pictures for your story.

There are many possible stories. Here is one about a camping trip.

Joe goes on a camping trip with his aunt, his uncle, and three cousins. They leave at 5:00 P.M. and drive 2 hours to the campground.

Joe helps his uncle put up three tents. His aunt cooks hamburgers on a grill that is over a fire.

In the morning, Joe tells his aunt that he is making pancakes for everyone. He decides to triple the recipe so there will be plenty of pancakes for everyone. A single recipe uses 2 cups of water, so he needs a total of 6 cups.

Pancake Mix
Recipe:
2 cups water
2 cups pancake mix
1/4 cup oil
1 egg
1/4 teaspoon salt

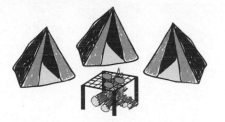

Joe's aunt has a 1-cup measuring cup and a ½-cup measuring cup. The water faucet is about 50 yards from the campsite. Joe tells his cousins that he can get 6 cups of water in only 4 trips.

When his cousins ask him how he knows that, he uses a stick to draw a diagram in the dirt. Joe says "This diagram shows that there are four 1½'s in 6. In other words,

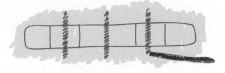

$$6 \div 1\frac{1}{2} = 4.$$

2.6 **Dividing Mixed Numbers** (continued)

2 **EXAMPLE:** Dividing by a Mixed Number

Show how Joe solves the division problem $6 \div 1\frac{1}{2}$ in Example 1.

3 **ACTIVITY:** Writing a Story

Work with a partner. Think of a story that uses division by a mixed number.

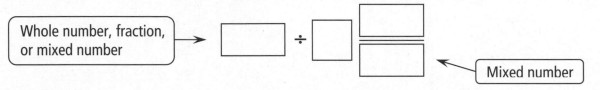

Whole number, fraction, or mixed number

÷

Mixed number

a. Write your story. Then draw pictures for your story.

b. Solve the division problem and use your answer in your story. Include a diagram of the division problem.

2.6 **Dividing Mixed Numbers** (continued)

What Is Your Answer?

4. IN YOUR OWN WORDS How can you use division by a mixed number as part of a story?

In Example 1, the units of the answer are *trips*.

$$\text{Cups} \div \frac{\text{Cups}}{\text{Trips}} = \text{Cups} \times \frac{\text{Trips}}{\text{Cups}}$$

$$= \cancel{\text{Cups}} \times \frac{\text{Trips}}{\cancel{\text{Cups}}}$$

$$= \text{Trips}$$

Find the units for the following division problems.

5. $\text{Miles} \div \dfrac{\text{Miles}}{\text{Hour}}$

6. $\text{Dollars} \div \dfrac{\text{Dollars}}{\text{Hour}}$

7. $\text{Miles} \div \text{Hour}$

8. $\text{Dollars} \div \text{Hour}$

Name _____ Date _____

Divide. Write the answer in simplest form.

1. $4\dfrac{1}{6} \div 5$

2. $\dfrac{5}{8} \div 5\dfrac{3}{4}$

3. $8\dfrac{1}{6} \div 2\dfrac{1}{24}$

Evaluate the expression when $x = 3\dfrac{3}{5}$ **and** $y = 6\dfrac{6}{7}$.

4. $2\dfrac{3}{10} \div x$

5. $y \div x$

6. $x \div y$

Evaluate the expression.

7. $4\dfrac{7}{12} \div \dfrac{3}{4} \times \dfrac{3}{11}$

8. $9 \div 8\dfrac{1}{10} - \dfrac{5}{9}$

9. $5\dfrac{7}{8} \times \left(2\dfrac{4}{5} \div 7\right)$

10. At a road race, you have $60\dfrac{3}{4}$ feet available for a water station. Your tables are $6\dfrac{3}{4}$ feet long. How many tables can you line up for the water station?

11. A recipe calls for $2\dfrac{2}{3}$ teaspoons of salt. You can only find three of your measuring spoons: a $\dfrac{1}{2}$ teaspoon, a $\dfrac{1}{8}$ teaspoon, and a $\dfrac{1}{6}$ teaspoon.

   a. What measuring spoon(s) would you use to measure the salt?

   b. How many scoops of each measuring spoon would you need?

2.7 Writing Decimals as Fractions
For use with Activity 2.7

Essential Question When you write a terminating decimal as a fraction, what type of denominator do you get?

A decimal that ends is called a **terminating decimal**. To convert a terminating decimal to a fraction, express the decimal in words.

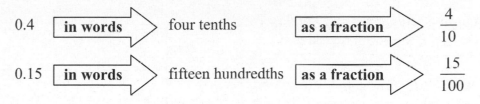

0.4   **in words**   four tenths   **as a fraction** $\dfrac{4}{10}$

0.15   **in words**   fifteen hundredths   **as a fraction** $\dfrac{15}{100}$

---

1 ACTIVITY: Writing Common Decimals as Fractions

Work with a partner. Complete the table.

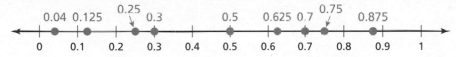

0.04 0.125 0.25 0.3 0.5 0.625 0.7 0.75 0.875

0   0.1   0.2   0.3   0.4   0.5   0.6   0.7   0.8   0.9   1

Decimal	Write as a Fraction	Simplify
0.04		
0.125		
0.25		
0.3		
0.5		
0.625		
0.7		
0.75		
0.875		

2.7 **Writing Decimals as Fractions** (continued)

2 ACTIVITY: 4 in a Row

Number of Players: 2

Work with a partner. Use the card shown.

- Each player should fill the squares of the card with decimals or simplified fractions from Activity 1. (Don't show your play card to the other player.)

- Players take turns calling out a fraction or decimal.

Both players cross out any number that is equal to the called out number.

The first person to get four numbers in the same row, column, or diagonal wins.

Check each other's work.

3 ACTIVITY: Vocabulary Patterns

Work with a partner. Match the word on the left with the description on the right.

Decimal   Originally the 10th month

Deciliter   A number system with base 10

December   Celebration of a 10th anniversary

Decennial   Ten years

Decade   One-tenth of a liter

Inductive Reasoning

4. a. Make a list of all the denominators you found in Activity 1.

2.7 **Writing Decimals as Fractions** (continued)

    b. Factor each denominator into prime factors.

    c. What similarities do you see in the denominators?

    d. Relate your answer to the decimal system.

5. Describe a good strategy you could use to win the game in Activity 2.

6. What does the prefix "dec" mean?

What Is Your Answer?

7. IN YOUR OWN WORDS When you write a terminating decimal as a fraction, what type of denominator do you get?

2.7 Practice
For use after Lesson 2.7

Write the decimal as a fraction or mixed number in simplest form.

1. 0.7

2. 0.282

3. 4.66

4. 2.125

Write the decimal as an improper fraction in simplest form.

5. 7.25

6. 5.32

7. 9.545

8. 4.118

9. You have 3.28 yards of fabric. The instructions for a project require $3\frac{2}{5}$ yards of fabric. Do you have enough fabric for the project? Explain.

10. You have to finish a race in $\frac{7}{8}$ of the time you ran in the semifinals in order to win. Your semifinal time was 25.6 seconds.

   a. Write your semifinal time as a mixed number in simplest form.

   b. What does your time need to be to win the race?

Name_____ Date_____

2.8 Writing Fractions as Decimals
For use with Activity 2.8

Essential Question How can you tell from the denominator of a fraction if its decimal form is terminating or repeating?

1 EXAMPLE: Writing a Fraction as a Decimal

Write the fraction as a decimal. Is it terminating or repeating?

a. $\dfrac{3}{8}$ b. $\dfrac{2}{3}$

Inductive Reasoning

Write the fraction as a decimal. Is it terminating or repeating?

2. $\dfrac{3}{4}$ 3. $\dfrac{1}{16}$

4. $\dfrac{1}{6}$ 5. $\dfrac{2}{9}$

2.8 **Writing Fractions as Decimals** (continued)

6. $\dfrac{7}{20}$

7. $\dfrac{7}{8}$

8. $\dfrac{5}{12}$

9. $\dfrac{21}{40}$

Use estimation to match the fraction with its decimal. Then use a calculator to check your answer.

10. $\dfrac{5}{6}$

11. $\dfrac{1}{3}$

12. $\dfrac{5}{8}$

13. $\dfrac{3}{16}$

A. 0.625

B. 0.1875

C. 0.333...

D. 0.83333...

14. In $\dfrac{1}{7} = 0.1428571428571428571\ldots$, what are the repeating digits? Can you find another fraction that has at least six digits that repeat?

What Is Your Answer?

15. Describe the denominators of fractions that can be written as

a. terminating decimals.

b. repeating decimals.

2.8 **Writing Fractions as Decimals** (continued)

16. **IN YOUR OWN WORDS** How can you tell from the denominator of a fraction if its decimal form is terminating or repeating?

17. **REASONING** The Mayan number system was base 20. In a base 20 system, describe the denominators of fractions that would be represented by terminating decimals and by repeating decimals.

0	1	2	3	4
5	6	7	8	9
10	11	12	13	14
15	16	17	18	19

18. **REASONING** The Babylonian number system was base 60. In a base 60 system, describe the denominators of fractions that would be represented by terminating decimals and by repeating decimals.

Name_____ Date _____

2.8 Practice
For use after Lesson 2.8

Write the fraction as a decimal.

1. $\dfrac{3}{4}$
2. $\dfrac{2}{5}$
3. $\dfrac{13}{15}$
4. $\dfrac{4}{3}$

Complete the statement using <, >, or =.

5. $\dfrac{4}{5}$ _____ 0.75
6. $\dfrac{7}{12}$ _____ 0.585

7. 0.72 _____ $\dfrac{18}{25}$
8. 0.56 _____ $\dfrac{17}{30}$

Write the number as a fraction. Then write the fraction as a decimal.

9. four-ninths
10. seven-tenths
11. twelve twenty-fifths

12. You travel $25\dfrac{1}{2}$ miles to a friend's house. Your odometer started at 13,520.8 miles. What will be your odometer reading when you reach your friend's house?

13. The table shows the jump distances for three long jumpers.

   a. Convert the jump distances to decimals. Then order the jump distances from least to greatest.

   b. How much farther is the distance for Jumper C than the distance for Jumper A?

Jumper	Jump Distance
A	$21\dfrac{5}{9}$ ft
B	$21\dfrac{5}{12}$ ft
C	$21\dfrac{11}{15}$ ft

Chapter 3 Fair Game Review

Find the product or quotient.

1. 351
    × 15

2. 187
    × 27

3. $9\overline{)333}$

4. $3\overline{)474}$

5. A bleacher row can seat 14 people. The bleachers are filled to capacity with 1330 people at a soccer game. How many rows of bleachers does the soccer field have?

6. A bus trip to New York City costs $166 per person. There are 52 people on the bus. How much money is collected for the trip?

Chapter 3 **Fair Game Review** (continued)

Find the sum or difference.

7. $1.48 + 0.057$

8. $2.52 + 8.94$

9. $3.087 + 0.12$

10. $6.02 + 7.9$

11. $3.8 - 2.01$

12. $5.46 - 4.9$

13. $7.183 - 0.066$

14. $6.58 - 0.008$

15. You buy a hat for \$12.95 and a pair of shoes for \$21.55. What is the total cost?

Name_____ Date _____

Essential Question   How can you use estimation to check that your answer is reasonable?

The newspaper ad shows the weekly specials at a grocery store.

---

1   ACTIVITY: Estimating a Decimal Sum

Work with a partner. You are buying the items on your shopping list.

- Find the *exact* total cost.

- *Estimate* the total cost.

- Use your estimate to check that your total is reasonable.

Shopping List

Hot Dogs
Bread
Potatoes
Cereal
Apples
Water

	Exact Cost	*Estimated Cost*
a. Hot Dogs		
Bread		
Potatoes		
Cereal		
Apples		
Water		

Is your estimate reasonable? If not, adjust your calculations.

3.1   **Decimals and Estimation** (continued)

Repeat the steps of part (a) for these lists.

b.
Shopping List

Crackers
Potatoes
Milk
Ketchup
Orange Juice

c.
Shopping List

Cereal
Bread
Eggs
Syrup
Apples

d.
Shopping List

Baby Food
Soup
Water
Ketchup
Hot Dogs

2 **ACTIVITY:** Estimating Decimal Products

You get home and realize you forgot to buy four boxes of crackers. Your friend says the crackers cost about $2.00 a box, so you should take $8.00.

  a. Fill in the blanks to show how   **b.** Find the actual total.
  your friend got the estimate.

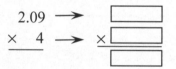

$$2.09 \rightarrow \boxed{}$$
$$\times\ \ 4 \rightarrow \times \boxed{}$$
$$\boxed{}$$

  c. What is wrong with your friend's estimate?

3 **ACTIVITY:** Writing a Story

Work with a partner. Write a story about the shopping list. As part of your story, imagine that the grocery clerk told you that the total was $137.56 and you used estimation to decide that the total was way too much.

Shopping List

2 Gallons Milk
3 Cartons Eggs
3 Boxes Cereal
Syrup
6 Cans Soup
2 Boxes Crackers

3.1 **Decimals and Estimation** (continued)

What Is Your Answer?

4. **IN YOUR OWN WORDS** How can you use estimation to check that your answer is reasonable?

5. The problems in the Activities are about groceries. Describe two other real-life examples in which estimation of decimals is useful.

6. In the cartoon, does Newton's rule work? Why does "lining up the decimal points" help when you are adding decimals?

"To add decimals I pretend I'm a top sergeant and say "All RIGHT you decimal points... LINE UP!"

7. Think of a cartoon that involves decimal addition or subtraction. Then draw the cartoon.

3.1 Practice
For use after Lesson 3.1

Estimate by rounding each factor to the nearest whole number.

1. 6×5.8

2. 9.07×3.33

3. $21.11 \div 6.73$

Use compatible numbers to estimate the product or quotient.

4. 19.57×4.86

5. $47.84 \div 11.99$

6. $65.58 \div 10.71$

Estimate the value of the expression.

7. $4.32 \times 9.44 \div 2.16$

8. $44.98 \div 4.86 \times 5.23$

9. $71.94 \div (1.85 \times 4.33)$

10. You and five friends go to a haunted house. Admission is $16.95 per person. Estimate how much tickets will cost for all of you. Is your estimate *too little* or *too much*? Explain.

11. You need four pieces of string that are 2.25 feet long to make a friendship bracelet. You have 20 feet of string.

    a. Estimate how much string you need to make one bracelet.

    b. Estimate how many bracelets you can make from the spool of string. Is your estimate *too little* or *too much*? Explain.

Name_____ Date_____

Essential Question What happens to the decimal point when you multiply a whole number by a decimal?

1 ACTIVITY: Multiplying by Powers of 10

Work with a partner. Complete the table. Then describe how to multiply by a power of 10.

Exponent	Power of 10	Product	Evaluate
1	$10^1 = 10$	10×0.825	8.25
2	$10^2 = 100$		
3	$10^3 = 1000$		
4	$10^4 = 10,000$		
5	$10^5 = 100,000$		

2 ACTIVITY: Multiplying a Decimal by a Whole Number

Work with a partner. Your school is selling tickets to the school carnival.

TICKETS: Only $0.25 EACH

a. Complete the table.

Number of Tickets	Price per Ticket	Find the Total	Total Cost
3	0.25	0.25 + 0.25 + 0.25	$0.75
4	0.25		
5	0.25		
15	0.25		
100	0.25		

3.2 **Multiplying Decimals and Whole Numbers** (continued)

b. The example in the table in part (a) shows how to find the total cost using addition. This works for small numbers of tickets. How did you find the total cost for the last two rows?

3 **ACTIVITY:** Back to School Shopping

Game Rules

- Take turns with your partner.

- When it is your turn, choose one item from the list. Decide whether you want to buy 1, 2, or 3 of your item. (Record your "purchases" on the next page.)

- The person who comes closest to $30 without going over, wins.

Back to School List

Item	Price	Item	Price
Ink Pens	$1.41	Paper Clips	$3.49
Pencils	$0.33	Markers	$3.29
Erasers	$0.24	Colored Pencils	$0.89
Poster Board	$0.64	Tissues	$2.29
Rulers	$1.99	Rubber Bands	$3.49
Protractors	$2.29	Notebook Paper	$3.98
Pocket Folders	$0.33	Graph Paper	$3.52
Sticky Notes	$0.99	Stapler	$12.63
Spirals	$1.15	Staples	$2.99
3-ring Binders	$4.26	Stickers	$0.99
Index Cards	$1.99	Calculator	$10.98
Scissors	$3.99	Book Covers	$1.15

3.2 Multiplying Decimals and Whole Numbers (continued)

Item	Item Price	Number of Items (1, 2, or 3)	Total

What Is Your Answer?

4. **IN YOUR OWN WORDS** What happens to the decimal point when you multiply a whole number by a decimal?

Name _____ Date _____

3.2 Practice
For use after Lesson 3.2

Find the product. Use an estimate to place the decimal point.

1. $\begin{array}{r} 0.5 \\ \times\ \ 4 \\ \hline \end{array}$

2. $\begin{array}{r} 0.9 \\ \times\ \ 7 \\ \hline \end{array}$

3. $\begin{array}{r} 3.8 \\ \times\ \ 6 \\ \hline \end{array}$

4. $\begin{array}{r} 2.1 \\ \times\ 11 \\ \hline \end{array}$

Multiply. Use estimation to check your answer.

5. 0.32×5

6. 7.81×2

7. 0.0046×9

Use the Distributive Property to rewrite the expression.

8. $3(a + 0.21)$

9. $4(x - 0.55)$

10. $12(k + 0.097)$

11. You use a microscope to look at bacteria that is 0.0034 millimeter long. The microscope magnifies the bacteria 430 times. How long does the bacteria appear to be when you look at it through the microscope?

12. Each weekday a bus travels 17.6 miles to school. How many miles does the bus travel to school and back in one week?

Name_____ Date_____

Essential Question When multiplying decimals, how do you know where to place the decimal point in the product?

1 EXAMPLE: Multiplying Decimals

Find 0.2×0.3.

_____   Write as fractions.

_____   Multiply the fractions.

_____   Rewrite the denominator as a power of 10.

_____   Rewrite the fraction as a decimal.

$0.2 \times 0.3 = $ _____.

2 ACTIVITY: Multiplying Decimals Using Powers of 10

Work with a partner.

   a. Complete the table. Use Example 1 as a model.

Problem	Rewrite as Fractions	Product	Denominator as Base 10	Rewrite as Decimal
0.2×3				
0.2×0.3				
0.2×0.03				
0.2×0.003				
0.2×0.0003				
0.2×0.00003				

3.3 **Multiplying Decimals** (continued)

b. Describe the connection between the first and last columns of the table in part (a).

3 **ACTIVITY:** Multiplying Decimals Using Powers of 10

Complete the table. Use Example 1 as a model.

Problem	Rewrite as Fractions	Product	Denominator as Base 10	Rewrite as Decimal
2×0.3				
0.2×0.3				
0.02×0.3				
0.002×0.3				
0.0002×0.3				

What Is Your Answer?

4. a. What differences do you notice between the tables in Activities 2 and 3?

b. What similarities do you notice?

3.3 **Multiplying Decimals** (continued)

5. **IN YOUR OWN WORDS** When multiplying decimals, how do you know where to place the decimal point in the product? Give examples in your description.

6. Write a general rule for multiplying two decimals. Give examples with your rule.

7. How many products can you find in the circle maze? List each product.

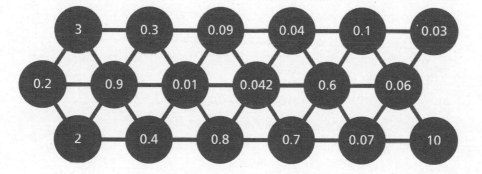

3.3 Practice
For use after Lesson 3.3

Multiply. Use estimation to check your product.

1. $\begin{array}{r} 0.8 \\ \times\, 0.6 \\ \hline \end{array}$

2. $\begin{array}{r} 0.003 \\ \times\, 0.09 \\ \hline \end{array}$

3. $\begin{array}{r} 8.91 \\ \times\, 1.26 \\ \hline \end{array}$

Evaluate the expression when $a = 4.8$, $b = 0.015$, and $c = 7.23$.

4. ab

5. $2.19c + 5.7$

6. $5.48a - 1.57$

Convert the fractions or mixed numbers to decimals. Then multiply.

7. $\dfrac{1}{8} \times \dfrac{3}{10}$

8. $\dfrac{17}{25} \times \dfrac{5}{16}$

9. $2\dfrac{31}{80} \times 4\dfrac{1}{2}$

10. You earn $7.80 an hour working as a dog sitter. You work 12.5 hours during the weekend. How much money do you make?

11. You buy a pair of shoes for $35.72 plus tax. The sales tax is found by multiplying the cost of the shoes by 0.06. What is the total cost of your purchase?

Name_____ Date_____

3.4 Dividing Decimals by Whole Numbers
For use with Activity 3.4

Essential Question How is dividing a decimal by a whole number similar to dividing a whole number by a whole number?

1 **ACTIVITY:** Dividing a Decimal by a Whole Number

Work with a partner. Use base ten blocks to model the division.

a. 3.2 ÷ 4

Begin by modeling 3.2 with base ten blocks. Sketch your model.

Next, think of 3.2 ÷ 4 as dividing 3.2 into four parts.
To do this, replace the ones blocks with tenths blocks.

How many tenths blocks do you have now? _____

Separate the blocks into four equal groups. Make a sketch of your groups.

There are four groups of _____ . So, 3.2 ÷ 4 = _____ .

3.4 **Dividing Decimals by Whole Numbers** (continued)

Use base ten blocks to find each quotient.

b. $1.2 \div 3$

c. $2.8 \div 4$

d. $2.6 \div 2$

e. $3.5 \div 5$

2 **ACTIVITY:** Where Does the Decimal Go?

Work with a partner. Use a pattern to complete each row. Use estimation to
check that your answer is reasonable.

a. $1236 \div 3 = 412$	$123.6 \div 3 = 41.2$	$12.36 \div 3 =$ _____	$1.236 \div 3 =$ _____
b. $5120 \div 10 = 512$	$512.0 \div 10 = 51.2$	$51.20 \div 10 =$ _____	$5.120 \div 10 =$ _____
c. $4 \div 2 = 2$	$0.4 \div 2 = 0.2$	$0.04 \div 2 =$ _____	$0.004 \div 2 =$ _____
d. $482.5 \div 1 = 482.5$	$482.5 \div 10 = 48.25$	$482.5 \div 100 =$ _____	$482.5 \div 1000 =$ _____
e. $10 \div 5 = 2$	$10 \div 50 = 0.2$	$10 \div 500 =$ _____	$10 \div 5000 =$ _____

Name_____ Date _____

3.4 **Dividing Decimals by Whole Numbers** (continued)

3 **ACTIVITY:** Using a Perimeter Formula

Work with a partner. Each shape has sides of equal length. Use the
perimeter to find the length of the sides. Write the formula and explain how
to find the length of the sides.

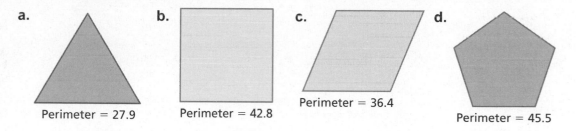

a. Perimeter = 27.9

b. Perimeter = 42.8

c. Perimeter = 36.4

d. Perimeter = 45.5

What Is Your Answer?

4. Which statements describe the division $13.5 \div 5$?

   a. How can you divide 13.5 into five equal parts?

   b. What is one-fifth of 13.5?

   c. How many fives are in 13.5?

5. **IN YOUR OWN WORDS** How is dividing a decimal by a whole number
   similar to dividing a whole number by a whole number? Use the patterns
   you found in Activity 2 to help write your answer. Give examples with
   your answer.

Name _____ Date _____

3.4 Practice
For use after Lesson 3.4

Divide. Check your answer.

1. $3\overline{)18.6}$

2. $6\overline{)46.8}$

3. $4\overline{)7.6}$

4. $24.5 \div 7$

5. $0.096 \div 8$

6. $15.65 \div 5$

Evaluate the expression.

7. $15.54 + 22.2 \div 6$

8. $59.85 \div 9 \times 8.23$

9. $10.02 \times (45.408 \div 3)$

10. You and three friends buy a birthday gift for a classmate. The gift costs $50.24. Each of you pays an equal amount for the gift. How much do you pay for the gift?

11. It costs $859.32 to have a school dance. Each ticket costs $8.

   a. How many tickets must be sold to cover the cost?

   School Dance

   October 28th
   Tickets $8

   b. How many tickets must be sold to make a $980.68 profit?

3.5 Dividing Decimals
For use with Activity 3.5

Essential Question How can you use base ten blocks to model decimal division?

1 ACTIVITY: Dividing Decimals

Work with a partner. Use base ten blocks to model the division.

a. Sample: $2.4 \div 0.6$

Begin by modeling 2.4 with base ten blocks. Sketch your model.

Next, think of the division $2.4 \div 0.6$ as the question "How many 0.6's are in 2.4?" To answer this, divide 2.4 into groups of 0.6 each.

Replace the ones blocks with tenths blocks.

How many tenths blocks do you have now? _____

Separate the blocks into groups of 0.6 each. Make a sketch of your groups.

There are _____ groups of 0.6. So, $2.4 \div 0.6 =$ _____.

3.5 **Dividing Decimals** (continued)

Use base ten blocks to find each quotient.

   b. 1.6 ÷ 0.8

   c. 2.8 ÷ 0.7

   d. 3.2 ÷ 0.4

   e. 3.6 ÷ 0.9

2 ACTIVITY: Dividing Decimals

Work with a partner. Use base ten blocks to model the division.

   a. Sample: 0.3 ÷ 0.06

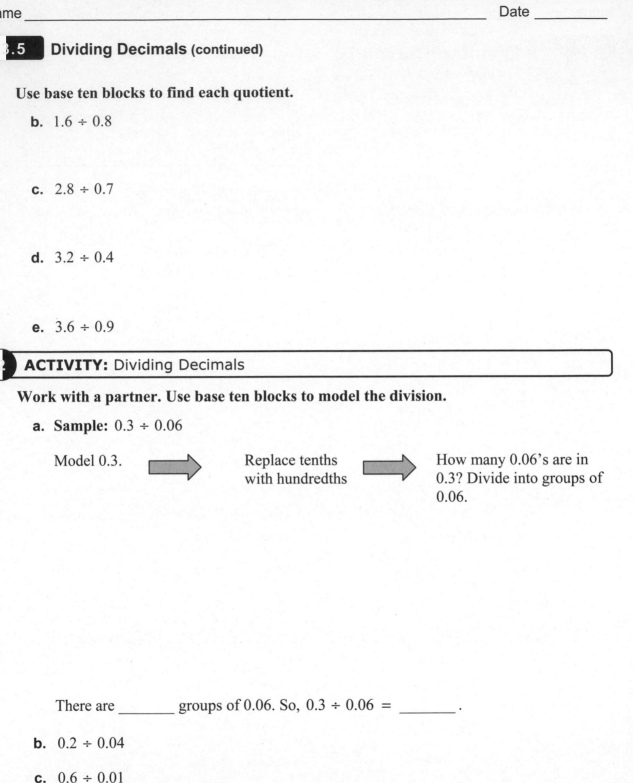

Model 0.3.   Replace tenths with hundredths   How many 0.06's are in 0.3? Divide into groups of 0.06.

There are _____ groups of 0.06. So, 0.3 ÷ 0.06 = _____ .

   b. 0.2 ÷ 0.04

   c. 0.6 ÷ 0.01

   d. 0.16 ÷ 0.08

   e. 0.28 ÷ 0.07

3.5 **Dividing Decimals** (continued)

What Is Your Answer?

3. **IN YOUR OWN WORDS** How can you use base ten blocks to model decimal division? Use examples from Activity 1 and Activity 2 as part of your answer.

4. **YOU BE THE TEACHER** Newton's poem is about dividing fractions. Write a poem about dividing decimals.

"When you must divide a fraction, do this very simple action:
Flip what you're dividing BY, and then it's easy—multiply!"

5. Think of your own cartoon about dividing decimals. Draw your cartoon.

3.5 Practice
For use after Lesson 3.5

Divide. Check your answer.

1. $3.1\overline{)17.36}$

2. $6.4\overline{)43.52}$

3. $7.05\overline{)8.46}$

4. $9.24 \div 15.4$

5. $7.06 \div 0.353$

6. $0.015 \div 0.003$

Without finding the quotient, complete the statement using <, >, or =.

7. $0.31 \div 0.062$ _____ $3.1 \div 6.2$

8. $10.68 \div 0.89$ _____ $1068 \div 89$

9. The tallest human height ever recorded is 8.925 feet tall. Your friend is 4.25 feet tall. How many times taller is the tallest human than your friend?

10. A plane travels 1020 miles from New York City to Minneapolis in 3.3 hours. The return trip takes 2.75 hours.

    a. How many times faster is the return trip?

    b. How fast is the plane flying in miles per hour during the return flight?

Fair Game Review

Write the decimal in words.

1. 0.8

2. 0.185

3. 1.67

4. 0.0506

Write the number as a decimal.

5. thirty-eight hundredths

6. seven hundred, twenty-four thousandths

7. nine ten thousandths

8. two and five tenths

9. For safety purposes, the dollar amount of a check is written in words. Write $15.87 in words.

```
                                                    2001

PAY TO THE
ORDER OF _____ $ [        ]
_____
                                               DOLLARS

        ☀ SUN
          SAVINGS BANK

MEMO _____    _____

⑆987654321⑆    123456789⑈    2001
```

Chapter 4 **Fair Game Review** (continued)

Use a number line to order the numbers from least to greatest.

10. 0.2, 0.54, 0.61, 0.4

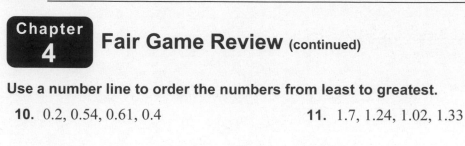

11. 1.7, 1.24, 1.02, 1.33

12. 0.98, 1.23, 0.87, 0.9

13. 0.003, 0.03, 0.033, 0.031

Write the decimal as a fraction or the fraction as a decimal.

14. 0.55

15. 0.242

16. $\dfrac{2}{5}$

17. $\dfrac{11}{16}$

18. In your class, 0.58 of the students bring a piece of whole fruit to lunch. Write the decimal as a fraction.

4.1 Percents and Fractions
For use with Activity 4.1

Essential Question How can you use a model to write a percent as a fraction or write a fraction as a percent?

1 **ACTIVITY:** Writing Percents as Fractions

Work with a partner. Write the percent shown by the model. Write the percent as a fraction with a denominator of 100. Simplify the fraction.

a. 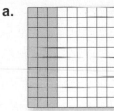   **b.**   **c.**

2 **ACTIVITY:** Writing Percents as Fractions

Work with a partner. Draw a model to represent the percent. Write the percent as a fraction with a denominator of 100. Simplify the fraction.

a. 60%   **b.** 5%   **c.** 85%   **d.** 28%

Name _____ Date _____

3 **ACTIVITY:** Writing Fractions as Percents

Work with a partner. Draw a model to represent the fraction. Rewrite the fraction with a denominator of 100. Write the fraction as a percent.

a. $\dfrac{2}{5}$

b. $\dfrac{7}{10}$ c. $\dfrac{3}{5}$

d. $\dfrac{3}{4}$ e. $\dfrac{3}{25}$

4.1 Percents and Fractions (continued)

What Is Your Answer?

4. **IN YOUR OWN WORDS** How can you use a model to write a percent as a fraction or write a fraction as a percent? Give an example with your answer.

5. Fractions that are terminating decimals are easier to write as percents than fractions that are repeating decimals. Write the percent shown by the model as a fraction. Explain your reasoning.

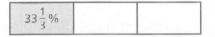

6. One way to answer a question about a percent is to write the percent as a fraction.

   a. Write the following question using a fraction.

      "How much is 50% of $2.00?"

   "Dear Sir, you could save a letter in writing 50% OFF by simply writing 50% ON."

   b. Use what you know about fractions to answer the question.

7. A notebook has an original price of $8.00. The notebook is on sale for 75% of the original price. Use a model to determine how much you will pay for the notebook.

4.1 Practice
For use after Lesson 4.1

Write the percent as a fraction or mixed number in simplest form.

1. 55%   2. 140%   3. 12.5%   4. 0.6%

Write the fraction or mixed number as a percent. Which method did you use?

5. $\dfrac{3}{4}$

6. $\dfrac{23}{40}$

7. $\dfrac{53}{200}$

8. $2\dfrac{7}{10}$

9. $8\dfrac{9}{25}$

10. $3\dfrac{11}{20}$

11. You answered 85% of the questions on the quiz correctly. What fraction of the questions did you answer correctly?

12. The states with the greatest number of electoral votes are shown in the table. There are 538 total electoral votes.

State	Electoral Votes
California	55
Texas	34
Indiana	11

    a. Each state's electoral votes represent what percent of the total electoral votes? Round your answers to the nearest tenth.

    b. California has about how many times more votes than Indiana?

4.2 Percents and Decimals
For use with Activity 4.2

Essential Question How does the decimal point move when you rewrite a percent as a decimal and when you rewrite a decimal as a percent?

1 ACTIVITY: Writing Percents as Decimals

Work with a partner. Write the percent shown by the model. Write the percent as a decimal.

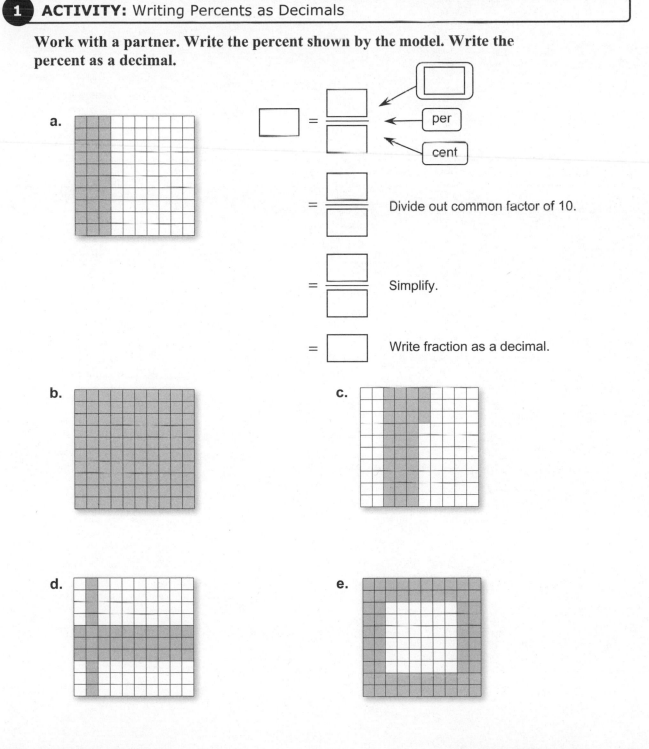

Divide out common factor of 10.

Simplify.

Write fraction as a decimal.

4.2 **Percents and Decimals** (continued)

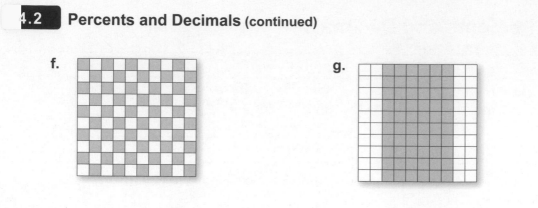

f.

g.

ACTIVITY: Writing Percents as Decimals

Work with a partner. Write the percent as a decimal.

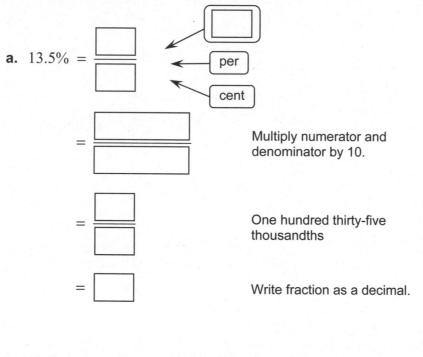

a. $13.5\% = \dfrac{\boxed{}}{\boxed{}}$

per

cent

$= \dfrac{\boxed{}}{\boxed{}}$ Multiply numerator and denominator by 10.

$= \dfrac{\boxed{}}{\boxed{}}$ One hundred thirty-five thousandths

$= \boxed{}$ Write fraction as a decimal.

b. 12.5% **c.** 3.8% **d.** 0.5%

4.2 **Percents and Decimals** (continued)

3 **ACTIVITY:** Writing Decimals as Percents

Work with a partner. Draw a model to represent the decimal. Write the decimal as a percent.

a. 0.1

b. 0.24

c. 0.58

d. 0.05

What Is Your Answer?

4. **IN YOUR OWN WORDS** How does the decimal point move when you rewrite a percent as a decimal and when you rewrite a decimal as a percent?

Name _____ Date _____

4.2 Practice
For use after Lesson 4.2

Write the percent as a decimal.

1. 35%

2. 160%

3. 74.8%

4. 0.3%

Write the decimal as a percent.

5. 1.23

6. 0.49

7. 0.024

8. 0.881

Write each percent as a fraction in simplest form and as a decimal.

9. 48%

10. 15.5%

11. 84.95%

12. People with severe hearing loss were given a sentence and word recognition test six months after they got implants in their ears. The patients scored an average of 82% on the test. Write this percent as a decimal.

13. Out of the first 15 serves in a volleyball game, 0.6 of them were in bounds.

   a. What percent of the serves were in bounds?

   b. What percent of the serves were not in bounds?

4.3 Comparing and Ordering Fractions, Decimals, and Percents For use with Activity 4.3

Essential Question How can you order numbers that are written as fractions, decimals, and percents?

1 ACTIVITY: Ordering Numbers

Work with a partner to order the following numbers.

$$\frac{1}{8} \qquad 11\% \qquad \frac{3}{20} \qquad 0.172 \qquad 0.32 \qquad 43\% \qquad 7\% \qquad 0.7 \qquad \frac{5}{6}$$

   a. Decide on a strategy for ordering the numbers. Will you write them all as fractions, decimals, or percents?

   b. Use your strategy and a number line to order the numbers from least to greatest. (Note: Label the number line appropriately.)

2 ACTIVITY: Using Fractions, Decimals, and Percents

Work with a partner. Decide which number form (fraction, decimal, or percent) is more common. Then find which is greater.

   a. 7% sales tax or $\frac{1}{20}$ sales tax

   b. 0.37 cup of flour or $\frac{1}{3}$ cup of flour

   c. $3\frac{5}{8}$-inch wrench or 3.69-inch wrench

   d. $12\frac{2}{3}$ dollars or 12.56 dollars

   e. 93% test score or $\frac{7}{8}$ test score

   f. $5\frac{5}{6}$ fluid ounces or 5.6 fluid ounces

4.3 **Comparing and Ordering Fractions, Decimals, and Percents** (continued)

---

3) **ACTIVITY:** The Game of Math Card War

Preparation:

- Cut index cards to make 40 playing cards.*

- Write each number in the table on a card.

75%	$\frac{3}{4}$	$\frac{1}{3}$	$\frac{3}{10}$	0.3	25%	0.4	0.25	100%	0.27
0.75	$66\frac{2}{3}\%$	12.5%	40%	$\frac{1}{4}$	4%	0.5%	0.04	$\frac{1}{100}$	$\frac{2}{3}$
0	30%	5%	$\frac{27}{100}$	0.05	$33\frac{1}{3}\%$	$\frac{2}{5}$	0.333...	27%	1%
1	0.01	$\frac{1}{20}$	$\frac{1}{8}$	0.125	$\frac{1}{25}$	$\frac{1}{200}$	0.005	0.666...	0%

To Play:

- Play with a partner.

- Deal 20 cards to each player face-down.

- Each player turns one card face-up. The player with the greater number wins. The winner collects both cards and places them at the bottom of his or her cards.

- Suppose there is a tie. Each player lays three cards face-down, then a new card face-up. The player with the greater of these new cards wins. The winner collects all ten cards and places them at the bottom of his or her cards.

- Continue playing until one player has all the cards. This player wins the game.

*Cut-outs are available in the back of the Record and Practice Journal.

4.3 **Comparing and Ordering Fractions, Decimals, and Percents** (continued)

What Is Your Answer?

4. **IN YOUR OWN WORDS** How can you order numbers that are written as fractions, decimals, and percents? Give an example with your answer.

5. All but one U.S. coin has a name that is related to its value. Which one is it? How are the names of the others related to their values?

Big Ideas Math Green **91**
Record and Practice Journal

Name _____ Date _____

4.3 Practice
For use after Lesson 4.3

Circle the number that is greater.

1. 0.06, 60%

2. 78%, $\dfrac{19}{25}$

3. $\dfrac{23}{20}$, 110%

4. 0.23, 2.3%

Use a number line to order the numbers from least to greatest.

5. 44.5%, 0.4445, $\dfrac{4}{9}$, 0.44

6. $\dfrac{5}{12}$, 0.4, 42%, 0.416

7. The table shows the portion of each age group that recycles plastic. Order the groups by the portion that recycle from least to greatest.

Age Group	Echo Boomers	Gen X	Baby Boomers	Matures
Portion that Recycle	51%	0.57	0.61	$\dfrac{6}{10}$

8. The table shows the portion of money spent on crafts annually in the United States. Order the portion of money spent from least to greatest.

Craft	Drawing	Painting	Scrapbooking	Home Decor
Portion of Money Spent	$\dfrac{1}{4}$	23.75%	0.325	$\dfrac{3}{16}$

Name_____ Date _____

Finding a Percent of a Number
For use with Activity 4.4

Essential Question How can you use mental math to find the percent of a number?

"I have a secret way for finding 21% of 80."

"10% is 8 and 1% is 0.8."

"So 21% is 8 + 8 + 0.8 = 16.8."

---

1 **EXAMPLE:** Finding 10% of a Number

a. How did Newton know that 10% of 80 is 8?

Write 10% as a fraction.

Method 1: Using a Model

0%	10%	20%	30%	40%	50%	60%	70%	80%	90%	100%
0	8	16	24	32	40	48	56	64	72	80

Method 2: Using Multiplication

b. How do you move the decimal point to find 10% of a number?

4.4 **Finding a Percent of a Number** (continued)

2 **ACTIVITY:** Finding 1% of a Number

Work with a partner.

   a. How did Newton know that 1% of 80 is 0.8?

   b. How do you move the decimal point to find 1% of a number?

3 **EXAMPLE:** Using Mental Math

Use mental math to find each percent of a number.

   a. 12% of 40   **b.** 19% of 50

4 **ACTIVITY:** Using Mental Math

Work with a partner. Use mental math to find each percent of a number.

   a. 20% tip for a $30 meal   **b.** 18% tip for a $30 meal

   c. 6% sales tax on a $20 shirt   **d.** 9% sales tax on a $20 shirt

4.4 **Finding a Percent of a Number** (continued)

    e. 6% commission on selling   **f.** 2% property tax on
       a $200,000 house   a $200,000 house

    g. 21% income tax on an   **h.** 38% income tax on an
       income of $40,000   income of $80,000

What Is Your Answer?

   5. **IN YOUR OWN WORDS** How can you use mental math to find the percent
      of a number?

   6. Describe two real-life examples of finding a percent of a number.

Name _____ Date _____

4.4 Practice
For use after Lesson 4.4

Find the percent of the number.

1. 30% of 50   2. 12% of 85   3. 2% of 96

4. 150% of 66   5. 7.5% of 120   6. 0.3% of 15

Complete the statement using <, >, or =.

7. 70% of 80 _____ 80% of 70   8. 92% of 30 _____ 48% of 75

9. You make homemade lip balm. About 11% of the lip balm is made from beeswax. You make $4\frac{2}{5}$ teaspoons of the lip balm. About how many teaspoons of beeswax do you need? Round your answer to the nearest tenth.

10. You score $\frac{63}{75}$ on your first test. After your second test, your teacher tells you your test average is 88%.

   a. The second test had 75 points possible. What percent did you receive on the second test?

   b. How many total points have you earned in the class?

Name_____ Date_____

4.5 Percents and Estimation
For use with Activity 4.5

Essential Question How can you use mental math and estimation to help solve real-life problems?

1 ACTIVITY: Estimating a Percent

Work with a partner. In the U.S. Constitution, the nation's capitol, Washington, D.C., was not allowed to exceed 10 miles square. After the capitol was built, it ended up having less than the maximum allowed area.

a. What was the maximum area allowed by the Constitution?

b. Use the grid to estimate the area of Washington, D.C. Explain your reasoning.

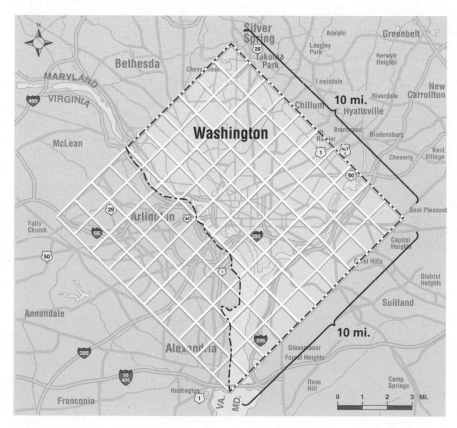

4.5 **Percents and Estimation** (continued)

c. What percent of the maximum allowed area did the capitol use?

$$\frac{\text{Actual Area}}{\text{Maximum Area Allowed}}$$

2 **EXAMPLE:** Using Mental Math

Use mental math to estimate each percent of a number.

a. 10% of $38.57

b. 19% of $71.33

10% of $38.57 is about _____.

19% of $71.33 is about _____.

3 **ACTIVITY:** Using Mental Math

Work with a partner. Use mental math to estimate each percent of a number. Use a calculator to check your estimate.

a. 20% tip for a $29.45 meal

b. 18% tip for a $29.45 meal

c. 6% sales tax on a $21.89 shirt

d. 9% sales tax on a $21.89 shirt

4.5 Percents and Estimation (continued)

e. 6% commission on selling
a $195,000 house

f. 2% property tax on
a $208,900 house

g. 21% income tax on an
income of $41,893.56

h. 38% income tax on an
income of $78,894.24

What Is Your Answer?

4. **IN YOUR OWN WORDS** How can you use mental math and estimation to
help solve real-life problems? Give two examples with your answer.

5. Estimate the percent of the U.S. flag that is
(a) red, (b) white, and (c) blue. Explain your
reasoning and include a diagram.

4.5 Practice
For use after Lesson 4.5

Estimate the percent of the number.

1. 19% of 22

2. 88% of 200

3. 26% of 81

4. 8% of 77

5. 73% of 41

6. 123% of 50

7. The gas mileage for your car is 22 miles to the gallon. After getting the car inspected and aligned, your gas mileage increases by 4%. About how much does your gas mileage increase?

8. You buy three shirts for a total of $64. The sales tax is 6% of the total price.

    a. Estimate how much your total will be with the sales tax.

    b. Estimate the average cost of each shirt after tax is added.

Chapter 5 Fair Game Review

Simplify the fraction.

1. $\dfrac{4}{10}$

2. $\dfrac{7}{35}$

3. $\dfrac{11}{88}$

4. $\dfrac{12}{18}$

5. $\dfrac{25}{45}$

6. $\dfrac{70}{120}$

7. There are 100 plants in a greenhouse. Thirty-eight of the plants are rose bushes. Write the fraction $\dfrac{38}{100}$ in simplest form.

Name _____ Date _____

In Exercises 8–10, use the double bar graph that shows the sales of a clothing store over two days.

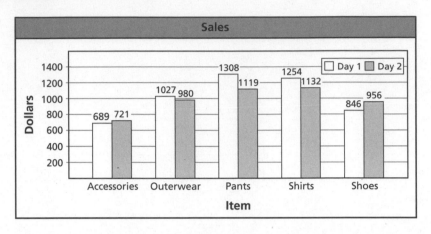

8. How much more did the store earn selling shirts on Day 1 than on Day 2?

9. Which item had the largest change in sales?

10. Which item had the highest sales total for the two days?

5.1 Ratios
For use with Activity 5.1

Essential Question   How can you tell whether two recipes make the same mixture?

A **ratio** is a comparison of two quantities using division.

Ratios

$$\frac{4 \text{ ft}}{2 \text{ ft}} \qquad \frac{3 \text{ c}}{5 \text{ c}} \qquad \frac{20 \text{ sec}}{45 \text{ sec}} \qquad \frac{120 \text{ mi}}{80 \text{ mi}}$$

 ACTIVITY: Comparing Recipes

Work with a partner.

You are making some homemade hand lotion. You find three recipes.

Do the recipes make the same lotion? How can you tell?

Recipe 1

Melt these ingredients over low heat:
2/3 cup of apricot oil
1/3 cup of cocoa butter
1 teaspoon of lanolin
1/2 ounce of grated beeswax

When cool, add the following:
2/3 cup of rosewater
1/3 cup of aloe vera gel
2 drops of rose oil
1 Vitamin E capsule

Whip together until the mixture resembles lotion.

Recipe 2

Melt these ingredients over low heat:
1 cup of apricot oil
1/2 cup of cocoa butter
1 1/2 teaspoons of lanolin
3/4 ounce of grated beeswax

When cool, add the following:
1 cup of rosewater
1/2 cup of aloe vera gel
3 drops of rose oil
1 1/2 Vitamin E capsules

Whip together until the mixture resembles lotion.

Recipe 3

Melt these ingredients over low heat:
1 1/2 cups of apricot oil
2/3 cup of cocoa butter
2 teaspoons of lanolin
1 ounce of grated beeswax

When cool, add the following:
1 1/2 cups of rosewater
2/3 cup of aloe vera gel
4 drops of rose oil
2 Vitamin E capsules

Whip together until the mixture resembles lotion.

Name _____ Date _____

2 **ACTIVITY:** Finding Equivalent Ratios

Work with a partner.

a. The ratios $\dfrac{1}{3}, \dfrac{2}{6}, \dfrac{3}{9}, \dfrac{4}{12}, \dfrac{5}{15}, \dfrac{6}{18}$ are all equivalent. Explain how you can use the multiplication table to show this.

	1	2	3	4	5	6	7	8	9	10	11	12
1	1	2	3	4	5	6	7	8	9	10	11	12
2	2	4	6	8	10	12	14	16	18	20	22	24
3	3	6	9	12	15	18	21	24	27	30	33	36
4	4	8	12	16	20	24	28	32	36	40	44	48
5	5	10	15	20	25	30	35	40	45	50	55	60
6	6	12	18	24	30	36	42	48	54	60	66	72
7	7	14	21	28	35	42	49	56	63	70	77	84
8	8	16	24	32	40	48	56	64	72	80	88	96
9	9	18	27	36	45	54	63	72	81	90	99	108
10	10	20	30	40	50	60	70	80	90	100	110	120
11	11	22	33	44	55	66	77	88	99	110	121	132
12	12	24	36	48	60	72	84	96	108	120	132	144

Use the multiplication table to find 10 more ratios that are equivalent to each ratio.

	Original Fraction										
b.	$\dfrac{2}{7}$										
c.	$\dfrac{8}{3}$										

5.1 **Ratios** (continued)

    d. Explain why the strategy in parts (a), (b), and (c) works to produce equivalent ratios.

What Is Your Answer?

3. You and two friends are making cookies. You make the original recipe amount. One of your friends makes a "half batch." Your other friend makes a "double batch." If you taste a spoonful of cookie dough from each batch, will they all taste the same? Explain your reasoning.

4. **IN YOUR OWN WORDS** How can you tell whether two recipes make the same mixture? Give an example.

Name _____   Date _____

Write the ratio in three ways. Explain what the ratio means.

1. forks to spoons

2. toothbrushes : toothpaste

   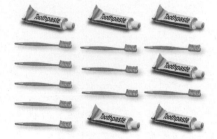

Write the ratio in simplest form.

3. $\dfrac{48}{36}$

4. $\dfrac{14}{50}$

5. $\dfrac{9}{72}$

Write two equivalent ratios for the given ratio.

6. $\dfrac{5}{20}$

7. $\dfrac{15}{7}$

8. $\dfrac{12}{60}$

9. There are 22 events at an indoor track and field meet. The ratio of track events to field events is 8 : 3. How many of the events are track events? Explain how you found your answer.

10. The directions for making orange juice from concentrate call for one part concentrate to three parts water. How much water is needed with four cans of concentrate?

5.2 Rates

For use with Activity 5.2

Essential Question How can you use rates to describe changes in real-life problems?

1 ACTIVITY: Stories Without Words

Work with a partner. Each diagram shows a story problem.

- Describe the story problem in your own words.

- Write the rate indicated by the diagram. What are the units?

- Rewrite the rate so that the denominator is 1. (This is a *unit rate*).

a.

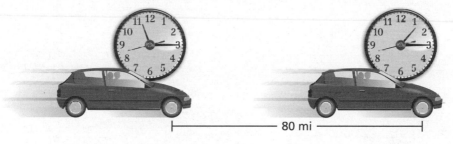

— 80 mi —

b.

5.2 **Rates** (continued)

c.

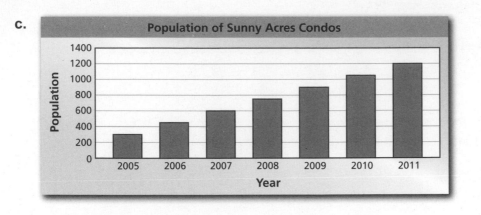

d.

January 2008
Length: 3 ft

January 2012
Length: 7 ft

---

2 **ACTIVITY:** Changing Units in a Rate

Work with a partner.

- **Change the units of the rate by multiplying by a "Magic One." Show your work.**

- **Write your answer as a unit rate.**

Original Rate		*Magic One*		*New Units*		*Unit Rate*

a. $\dfrac{\$120}{h}$ $\times$ $\dfrac{\boxed{}}{\boxed{}}$ $=$ $\dfrac{\boxed{}}{\boxed{}}$ $=$ $\dfrac{\$\boxed{}}{1\ \text{min}}$

Name_____ Date_____

b. $\dfrac{\$3}{\text{min}}$ × $\dfrac{\boxed{}}{\boxed{}}$ = $\dfrac{\boxed{}}{\boxed{}}$ = $\dfrac{\$\boxed{}}{1\ \text{h}}$

c. $\dfrac{36\ \text{people}}{\text{yr}}$ × $\dfrac{\boxed{}}{\boxed{}}$ = $\dfrac{\boxed{}}{\boxed{}}$ = $\dfrac{\boxed{}\ \text{people}}{1\ \text{mo}}$

d. $\dfrac{12\ \text{in.}}{\text{ft}}$ × $\dfrac{\boxed{}}{\boxed{}}$ = $\dfrac{\boxed{}}{\boxed{}}$ = $\dfrac{\boxed{}\ \text{in.}}{1\ \text{yd}}$

e. $\dfrac{60\ \text{mi}}{\text{h}}$ × $\dfrac{\boxed{}}{\boxed{}}$ = $\dfrac{\boxed{}}{\boxed{}}$ = $\dfrac{\boxed{}\ \text{mi}}{1\ \text{min}}$

f. $\dfrac{2\ \text{ft}}{\text{week}}$ × $\dfrac{\boxed{}}{\boxed{}}$ = $\dfrac{\boxed{}}{\boxed{}}$ = $\dfrac{\boxed{}\ \text{ft}}{1\ \text{yr}}$

What Is Your Answer?

3. One problem-solving strategy is called *Working Backwards*. What does this mean? How can this strategy be used to find the rates in Activity 2?

4. **IN YOUR OWN WORDS** How can you use rates to describe changes in real-life problems? Give two examples.

Name _____ Date _____

 Practice
5.2 For use after Lesson 5.2

Write a rate that represents the situation.

1. 110 calories in 20 minutes

2. $5.00 for 2 boxes

Write a unit rate for the situation.

3. 9 strikes in 3 innings

4. 117 points in 13 minutes

Decide whether the rates are equivalent.

5. $\dfrac{30 \text{ beats}}{20 \text{ seconds}}, \dfrac{90 \text{ beats}}{60 \text{ seconds}}$

6. $\dfrac{15 \text{ pages}}{20 \text{ minutes}}, \dfrac{10 \text{ pages}}{15 \text{ minutes}}$

7. One of the valves on the Hoover Dam releases 40,000 gallons of water per second. What is the rate, in gallons per minute?

8. A 12-pack of water costs $3.90. A 20-pack of water costs $5.60.

   a. Which is the better buy? Why?

   b. You need to buy water for 60 people. How much money will you save by buying the better buy?

5.3 Solving Rate Problems
For use with Activity 5.3

Essential Question How can you use rates to help show how a country can save valuable natural resources?

> *For want of a nail the shoe was lost.*
>
> *For want of a shoe the horse was lost.*
>
> *For want of a horse the rider was lost.*
>
> *For want of a rider the battle was lost.*
>
> *For want of a battle the kingdom was lost.*
>
> *—And all for the want of a horseshoe nail.*

 1 ACTIVITY: Saving Water

The nursery rhyme above is an example of how a small problem can lead to a big problem.

Work with a partner. Here is an example about a leaky faucet that drips a drop of water every 2 seconds.

a. Complete the table showing how many drops of water drip in different amounts of time. Write each entry in the table as a rate in drops per unit of time.

Drops	1					
Time	2 sec	1 min	1 h	1 d	1 wk	1 yr

b. How many gallons of water are wasted in a year? Show your work.

> 80 drops = 1 teaspoon
> 96 teaspoons = 1 pint
> 8 pints = 1 gallon

5.3 Solving Rate Problems (continued)

c. There are about 125 million homes and apartments in the United States. Suppose every one of them has a leaky faucet. How many gallons of water will be wasted each year? Explain your reasoning.

d. The swimming pool shown at the right holds about 15,000 gallons of water. How many times could this pool be filled by the amount of water you found in part (c)?

4 ft

36 ft

14 ft

2 ACTIVITY: Saving Gasoline

Work with a partner.

Drivers in the United States use about 400 million gallons of gasoline each day. There are about 250 million automobiles in the United States. The typical fuel economy of automobiles is about 17 miles per gallon.

Compact
32 mpg City
40 mpg Highway

10.3 gallon tank

Full Size
20 mpg City
29 mpg Highway

17.5 gallon tank

SUV
13 mpg City
17 mpg Highway

25.0 gallon tank

5.3 **Solving Rate Problems** (continued)

a. How much gas does the typical automobile in the United States use each day?

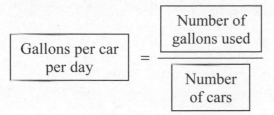

b. How many miles is a typical automobile in the United States driven each day?

$$\boxed{\begin{array}{c}\text{Miles per car}\\\text{per day}\end{array}} = \boxed{\begin{array}{c}\text{Gallons per car}\\\text{per day}\end{array}} \times \boxed{\text{Fuel economy}}$$

c. How much gas can be saved each day by increasing the typical fuel economy in the United States to 25 miles per gallon? Explain your reasoning.

What Is Your Answer?

3. **IN YOUR OWN WORDS** How can you use rates to help show how a country can save valuable natural resources? Give an example.

4. **RESEARCH** In Activities 1 and 2, rates are used to show how to save water and gasoline. Think of another example in which rates can be used in efforts to save a natural resource.

Name _____ Date _____

Find the distance.

1. $d =$ _____, $r = 45$ mi/h, $t = 5$ h   2. $d =$ _____, $r = 7$ ft/sec, $t = 12$ sec

Find the speed.

3. 200 meters in 25 seconds   4. 250 miles in 4 hours

Find how far the object travels in the given amount of time.

5. 10 hours   6. 3 minutes

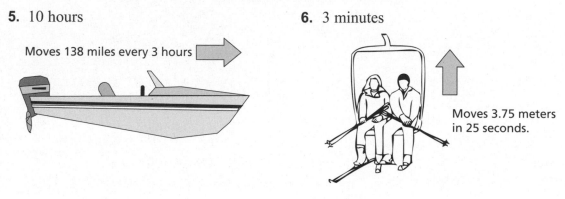

Moves 138 miles every 3 hours

Moves 3.75 meters in 25 seconds.

7. You can type 115 words in three minutes. About how many words can you type in seven minutes?

8. You leave your house at 1 P.M. to go to a wedding. The ceremony starts at 5 P.M. and is 350 miles away. You drive 65 miles per hour. Will you make it to the wedding on time? If so, how much time do you have to spare? If not, how late will you be?

5.4 Mean
For use with Activity 5.4

Essential Question What is the meaning of the word "average?" How can you find the average of a collection of numbers?

---

1 ACTIVITY: Describing an Average

Work with a partner. A women's shoe store is analyzing its stock. The bar graph shows the percent of women's shoes in stock for each size.

a. What percent of the shoes are size $7\frac{1}{2}$, 8, or $8\frac{1}{2}$?

Women's Shoes

Percent (y-axis: 0, 2, 4, 6, 8, 10, 12, 14, 16)

Shoe Size (x-axis: $4\frac{1}{2}$, 5, $5\frac{1}{2}$, 6, $6\frac{1}{2}$, 7, $7\frac{1}{2}$, 8, $8\frac{1}{2}$, 9, $9\frac{1}{2}$, 10, $10\frac{1}{2}$, 11, $11\frac{1}{2}$)

b. There are 200 pairs of shoes in stock. How many are size 7? Explain your reasoning.

c. What is the average shoe size for the shoes in stock? Explain.

---

2 ACTIVITY: Describing a Collection of Shoe Sizes

Work with a partner. A women's shoe store has 20 customers with the following sizes.

$6\frac{1}{2}$ 8   9   7   7   6   10   8 $8\frac{1}{2}$ 11

$7\frac{1}{2}$ $8\frac{1}{2}$ 8   7   8 $5\frac{1}{2}$ 6   9   8 $8\frac{1}{2}$

5.4 **Mean** (continued)

a. Use a table or a graph to organize the shoe sizes of the 20 customers.

b. Write a short paragraph describing the shoe sizes.

c. Is the entire stock in the shoe store, as shown in Activity 1, well represented by these 20 customers?

---

3 **ACTIVITY:** Talking About Averages

Work with a partner. Talk about the statement. What type of survey or research do you think was done to write each statement?

a. The average height for men in the United States is 5 feet, 9 inches.

b. The average annual income for a family in the United States is $52,000.

c. The average fuel economy for a car in the United States is 17 miles per gallon.

d. The average age of a person living in the United States is 36.4 years.

5.4   **Mean** (continued)

    e. The average amount of dog food eaten by a dog in the United States is 1.2 pounds per day.

What Is Your Answer?

  4. IN YOUR OWN WORDS What is the meaning of the word "average?" How can you find the average of a collection of numbers? Give two examples of averages.

  5. There are 5 students in the cartoon. Four of the students are 66 inches tall. One is 96 inches tall.

"Yup, the average height in our class is 6 feet."

    a. How do you think the students decided their average height is 6 feet?

    b. Does a height of 6 feet seem like a good representation of the average height of the 5 students? Explain why or why not.

Name _____ Date _____

Find the mean of the data.

1. Emails sent in the last 4 hours:
   2, 5, 4, 5

2. Magazine subscriptions sold this week:
   3, 6, 7, 6, 7, 9, 11

3.

Books Brought Home	
Monday	|
Tuesday	|||
Wednesday	||||
Thursday	||||
Friday	|

4. The table shows the number of points scored by your team in each quarter of a football game. What is the mean number of points scored in a quarter?

Quarter	1	2	3	4
Points	3	14	10	0

5. A group of 12 students has a mean height of 58 inches. Another group of 6 students has a mean height of 52 inches. What is the mean height of the 18 students? Explain how you found your answer.

Name_____ Date_____

Essential Question Describe situations in real life where the mean is not a good representation of the average.

1 **ACTIVITY:** Comparing Three Samples

Work with a partner. Surveys are taken in three grade 6–12 schools. Make up a story about the three surveys. Find the mean for each survey. Do you think the mean is a good way to represent the "average" of each group? Why or why not?

a.

5.5 **Median, Mode, and Range** (continued)

b.

c.

5.5   **Median, Mode, and Range** (continued)

2   **ACTIVITY:** When the Mean is Misleading

Work with a partner. Read and re-read each statement. Think of a better way to represent the "average" so that the statement is not so misleading.

a. Someone is trying to criticize a small high school by saying "Last year, the average age of the graduating class was 22 years old." When you look into the facts, you find that the class had a senior citizen who went back to school to earn a diploma. Here are the ages for the class.

18, 18, 18, 18, 18, 17, 18, 19, 18 ,18, 18, 18, 18, 74

What percent of the ages are *below* the mean?

b. There is a small town where most of the people are having a difficult time getting by because of low incomes. Someone is trying to ignore the problem and writes an article in the newspaper saying "It is not so bad in the town. The average income for a family is $52,000 a year." Here are the incomes.

$20,000, $20,000, $20,000, $20,000, $30,000, $30,000, $30,000, $30,000, $40,000, $40,000, $40,000, $50,000, $50,000, $50,000, $310,000

What percent of families have incomes *below* the mean?

What Is Your Answer?

3. **IN YOUR OWN WORDS** Describe situations in real life where the mean is not a good representation of the average. What measures (other than mean) can you use to describe an average?

5.5 **Practice**
For use after Lesson 5.5

Find the median, mode(s), and range of the data.

1. 3, 2, 3, 6, 7, 5, 9

2. 12, 14, 15, 13, 12, 12, 15, 10, 14

3. 15, 53, 34, 64, 28, 79, 66, 41

4. 3.4, 7.5, 8.8, 9.2, 3.4, 5.1, 7.5, 2.4, 8.3, 7.6

5. Find the median, mode, and range of the number of dots in the Braille alphabet. Explain how you found your answers.

The Braille Alphabet

a	b	c	d	e	f	g	h	i	j

k	l	m	n	o	p	q	r	s	t

u	v	w	x	y	z

6. Your quiz scores are 17, 17, 16, 20, 18, 19, 17, 14, 19, and 20. Your teacher drops the lowest quiz score. How are the mean, median, mode, and range of the points affected?

5.6 **Analyzing Data Sets**
For use with Activity 5.6

Essential Question How can you use tables and graphs to help organize data?

1 **ACTIVITY:** Conducting an Experiment

Work with a partner.

a. Roll a number cube 20 times. Record your results in a tally chart.

	1	2	3	4	5	6
Tally						

Key: | = 1   ⍓⍓ = 5

b. Make a bar graph of your totals.

c. Go to the board and enter your totals in the class tally chart.

d. Make a second bar graph showing the class totals. Compare and contrast the two bar graphs.

5.6 **Analyzing Data Sets** (continued)

2 **ACTIVITY:** Organizing Data

Work with a partner. You are judging a paper airplane contest. Each contestant flies his or her paper airplane 20 times. Make a tally chart and a graph of the distances.

Complete the table and the graph using the data shown.

20.5 ft, 24.5 ft, 18.5 ft, 19.5 ft, 21.0 ft, 14.0 ft, 12.5 ft, 20.5 ft, 17.5 ft, 24.9 ft,
19.5 ft, 17.0 ft, 18.5 ft, 12.0 ft, 21.5 ft, 23.0 ft, 13.5 ft, 19.0 ft, 22.5 ft, 19.0 ft

Interval	Tally	Total
10.0–12.9		
13.0–15.9		
16.0–18.9		
19.0–21.9		
22.0–24.9		

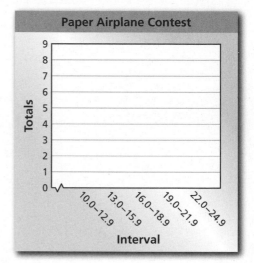

a. Make a different tally chart and graph of the distances using the following intervals.

10.0–11.9, 12.0–13.9, 14.0–15.9, 16.0–17.9,
18.0–19.9, 20.0–21.9, 22.0–23.9, 24.0–25.9

5.6 Analyzing Data Sets (continued)

b. Which graph do you think represents the distances better? Explain.

3 **ACTIVITY:** Developing an Experiment

Work with a partner.

a. Design and make a paper airplane from a single sheet of $8\frac{1}{2}$-by-11 inch paper.

b. Fly the airplane 20 times. Keep track of the distance flown each time.

Flight	1	2	3	4	5	6	7	8	9	10
Distance										
Flight	11	12	13	14	15	16	17	18	19	20
Distance										

c. Organize your results in a tally chart and a graph. What is the mean distance flown by the airplane?

What Is Your Answer?

4. IN YOUR OWN WORDS How can you use tables and graphs to help organize data? Give examples of careers in which the organization of data is important.

Name _____ Date _____

Practice
For use after Lesson 5.6

Find the mean, median, and mode(s) of the data. Choose the measure that best represents the data. Explain your reasoning.

1. 2, 32, 35, 35, 38, 29

2. 14, 26, 45, 43, 57

Find the mean, median, and mode(s) of the data with and without the outlier. Describe the effect of the outlier on the measures of central tendency.

3. 4, 15, 6, 12, 68, 12

4. 0, 54, 62, 64, 55, 55, 54, 62

5. The data show your strokes for 18 holes of miniature golf.
   4, 5, 3, 3, 1, 2, 3, 2, 4, 8, 2, 4, 4, 5, 2, 3, 6, 2
   Find the mean, median, and mode(s) of the data. Which measure best represents the data? Explain your reasoning.

6. The table shows the amount of time you spend practicing the piano in a week.

Day	Sun	Mon	Tues	Wed	Thurs	Fri	Sat
Time (minutes)	0	30	20	40	40	20	40

   Which measure best represents the data? Explain your reasoning.

Name_____ Date_____

 Practice
For use after Lesson 5.6b

Display the data in a line plot. Describe the distribution of the data.

1.

Games Won				
9	8	9	8	7
10	9	8	4	8
9	7	3	9	7

2.

Number of Students				
14	10	15	14	9
15	12	14	11	10
11	13	9	13	12

Display the data in a histogram.

3.

Zoo Admission	
Age	Frequency
3–5	16
6–8	21
9–11	25
12–14	19
15–17	8

4.

Confirmed Flu Cases per School	
Cases	Frequency
0–2	3
3–5	7
6–8	9
9–11	12

Name _____ Date _____

Make a box-and-whisker plot for the data.

5. Number of song downloads:
4, 2, 6, 1, 5, 4, 5, 2, 3, 4

6. Number of text messages sent:
7, 3, 9, 12, 8, 7, 3, 9, 8

7. The box-and-whisker plot shows the number of children enrolling in summer camp.

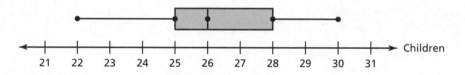

a. What portion of summer camp enrollment is 25 children or less?

b. What portion of summer camp enrollment is between 25 children and 30 children?

c. Find and interpret the interquartile range of data.

Name_____ Date_____

Identify the basic shapes in the figure.

1.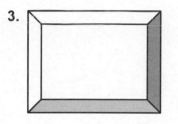

2.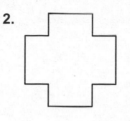

3.
   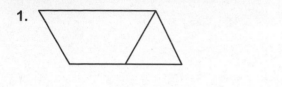

4.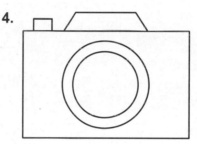

5. Identify the basic shapes that make up the top of your teacher's desk.

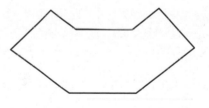

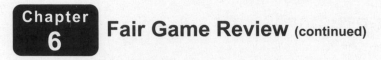

Chapter 6 **Fair Game Review** (continued)

Evaluate the expression.

6. 7^2
7. 11^2
8. $4(5)^2$

9. $7 \bullet 10^2$
10. $4(4 + 2)^2$
11. $5(6 + 3)^2$

12. $6(8 + 3)^2 + 2 \bullet 9$
13. $4(12)^2 - (6 + 4)$

14. A kilometer is 10^3 meters. You run a 5 kilometer race. How many meters do you run?

6.1 Circles and Circumference
For use with Activity 6.1

Essential Question How can you find the circumference of a circle?

Archimedes was a Greek mathematician, physicist, engineer, and astronomer.

Archimedes discovered that in any circle the ratio of circumference to diameter is always the same. Archimedes called this ratio pi, or π (a letter from the Greek alphabet).

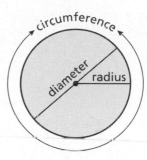

$$\pi = \frac{\text{Circumference}}{\text{Diameter}}$$

In Activities 1 and 2, you will use the same strategy Archimedes used to approximate π.

---

1 ACTIVITY: Approximating Pi

Work with a partner. Record your results in the first row of the table on the next page.

- Measure the perimeter of the large square in millimeters.

- Measure the diameter of the circle in millimeters.

- Measure the perimeter of the small square in millimeters.

- Calculate the ratios of the two perimeters to the diameter.

- The average of these two ratios is an approximation of π.

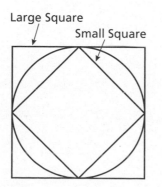

6.1 Circles and Circumference (continued)

Sides of Polygon	Large Perimeter	Diameter of Circle	Small Perimeter	Large Perimeter / Diameter	Small Perimeter / Diameter	Average of Ratios
4						
6						
8						
10						

2 ACTIVITY: Approximating Pi

Continue your approximation of pi. Complete the table on the previous page using a hexagon (6 sides), an octagon (8 sides), and a decagon (10 sides).

a. Large Hexagon

Small Hexagon

b. Large Octagon

Small Octagon

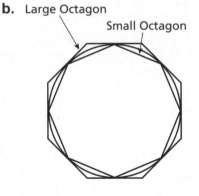

c. Large Decagon

Small Decagon

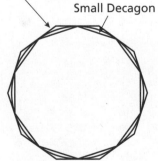

6.1 Circles and Circumference (continued)

d. From the table, what can you conclude about the value of π? Explain your reasoning.

e. Archimedes calculated the value of π using polygons having 96 sides. Do you think his calculations were more or less accurate than yours?

What Is Your Answer?

3. **IN YOUR OWN WORDS** Now that you know an approximation for pi, explain how you can use it to find the circumference of a circle. Write a formula for the circumference C of a circle whose diameter is d. Draw a circle and use your formula to find the circumference.

6.1 Practice
For use after Lesson 6.1

1. Find the diameter of the circle.

9 in.

2. Find the radius of the circle.

12 in.

Find the circumference of the circle. Use 3.14 or $\frac{22}{7}$ for π.

3.

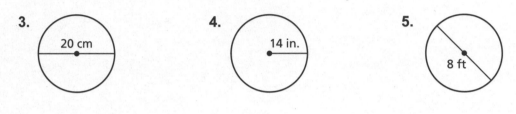

20 cm

4.

14 in.

5.

8 ft

Find the perimeter of the semicircular region.

6.

5 in.

7.

21 ft

8. A simple impact crater on the moon has a diameter of 15 kilometers. A complex impact crater has a radius of 30 kilometers. How much greater is the circumference of the complex impact crater than the simple impact crater?

Name_____ Date_____

6.2 Perimeters of Composite Figures
For use with Activity 6.2

Essential Question How can you find the perimeter of a composite figure?

1 ACTIVITY: Finding a Pattern

Work with a partner. Describe the pattern of the perimeters. Use your pattern to find the perimeter of the tenth figure in the sequence. (Each small square has a perimeter of 4).

a.

b.

c.

6.2 Perimeters of Composite Figures (continued)

2 ACTIVITY: Finding a Distance

Work with a partner.

   a. Estimate the distance to the gold.

   b. Estimate the distance to the silver.

3 ACTIVITY: Submitting a Bid

Work with a partner. You want to bid on a tiling contract. You will be supplying and installing the tile that borders the swimming pool shown on the next page.

   • Your cost for the tile is $4 per linear foot.

   • It takes about 15 minutes to prepare, install, and clean each foot of tile.

   a. How many tiles are needed for the border?

6.2 **Perimeters of Composite Figures** (continued)

b. Write a bid for how much you will charge to supply and install the tile. Include what you want to charge as an hourly wage. Estimate what you think your profit will be.

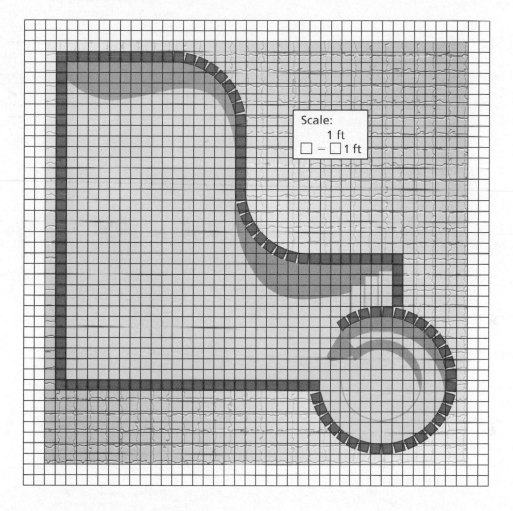

Scale:
1 ft
□ – □ 1 ft

What Is Your Answer?

4. IN YOUR OWN WORDS How can you find the perimeter of a composite figure? Use a semicircle, a triangle, and a parallelogram to draw a composite figure. Label the dimensions. Find the perimeter of the figure.

6.2 Practice
For use after Lesson 6.2

Each square on the grid paper is 1 square inch. Estimate the perimeter of the figure.

1.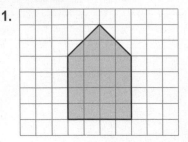

2.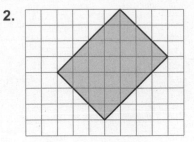

Find the perimeter of the figure.

3.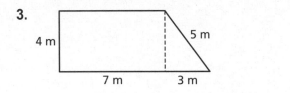

4.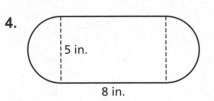

5. You are having a swimming pool installed.

   a. Find the perimeter of the swimming pool.

   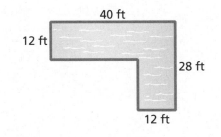

   b. Tiling costs $15 per yard. How much will it cost to put tiles along the edge of the pool?

Name_____ Date_____

6.3 Areas of Circles
For use with Activity 6.3

Essential Question How can you find the area of a circle?

1 ACTIVITY: Estimating the Area of a Circle

Work with a partner. Each square in the grid is 1 unit by 1 unit.

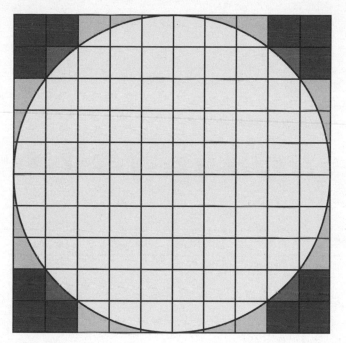

a. Find the area of the large 10-by-10 square.

b. Complete the table.

Region Outside of Circle			
Area			

c. Use your results to approximate the area of the circle. Explain your reasoning.

6.3   **Areas of Circles** (continued)

    d. Fill in the blanks. Explain your reasoning.

$$\text{Area of large square} = \underline{\hspace{1.5cm}} \cdot 5^2$$

$$\text{Area of circle} = \underline{\hspace{1.5cm}} \cdot 5^2$$

    e. What can you conclude?

 2 **ACTIVITY:** Approximating the Area of a Circle

Work with a partner.

    a. Draw a circle. Label the radius as r.*

    b. Divide the circle into 24 equal sections.

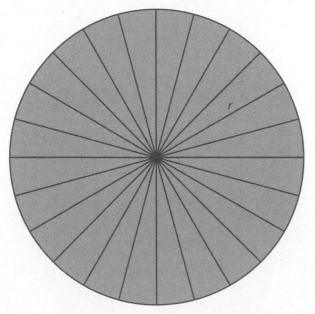

    *Cut-outs are available in the back of the Record and Practice Journal.

6.3 **Areas of Circles** (continued)

c. Cut the sections apart. Then arrange them to approximate a parallelogram.

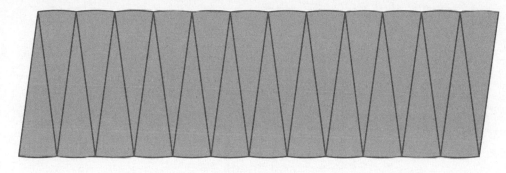

d. What is the approximate height and base of the parallelogram?

e. Find the area of the parallelogram. What can you conclude?

What Is Your Answer?

3. **IN YOUR OWN WORDS** How can you find the area of a circle?

4. Write a formula for the area of a circle with radius *r*. Find an object that is circular. Use your formula to find the area.

Name _____ Date _____

Find the area of the circle. Use 3.14 or $\frac{22}{7}$ for π.

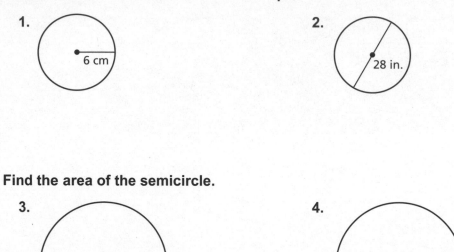

1.

    6 cm

2.

    28 in.

Find the area of the semicircle.

3.

    18 in.

4.

    30 ft

5. An FM radio station signal travels in a 40-mile radius. An AM radio station signal travels in a 4-mile radius. How much more area does the FM station cover than the AM station?

6. A sprinkler at a golf course is set to spray in a semicircle. The sprinkler can spray water a distance of 25 feet. What is the area of the golf course that is watered by the sprinkler?

6.4 Areas of Composite Figures
For use with Activity 6.4

Essential Question   How can you find the area of a composite figure?

1 **ACTIVITY:** Estimating Area

Work with a partner.

   a. Choose a state. On grid paper, draw a larger outline of the state.

   b. Use your drawing to estimate the area (in square miles) of the state.

   c. Which state areas are easy to find? Which are difficult? Why?

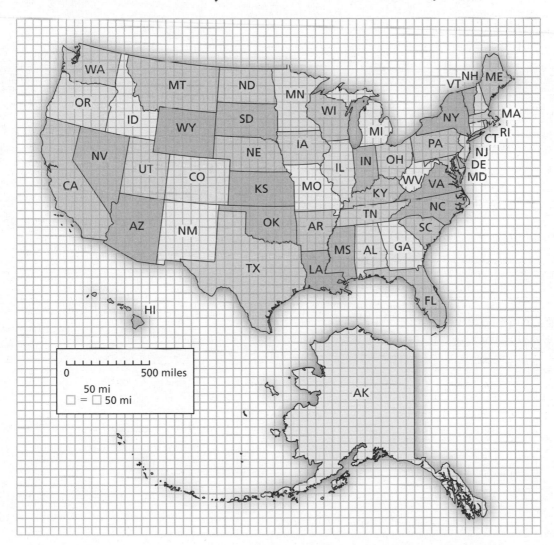

6.4 **Areas of Composite Figures** (continued)

2 **ACTIVITY:** Estimating Areas

Work with a partner. The completed puzzle has an area of 150 square centimeters.*

  a. Estimate the area of each puzzle piece.

  b. Check your work by adding the six areas. Why is this a check?

3 **ACTIVITY:** Filling a Square with Circles

Work with a partner. Look at patterns (a)–(d). Which pattern fills more of the square with circles? Explain.

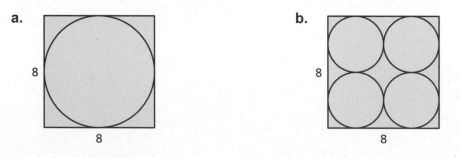

   a.

8

8

   b.

8

8

*Cut-outs are available in the back of the Record and Practice Journal.

6.4 **Areas of Composite Figures** (continued)

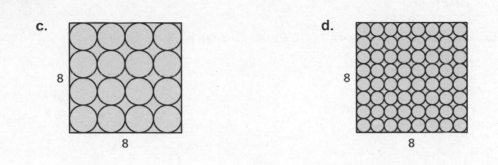

c.

8

8

d.

8

8

What Is Your Answer?

4. **IN YOUR OWN WORDS** How can you find the area of a composite figure?

5. Summarize the area formulas for all the basic figures you have studied. Draw a single composite figure that has each type of basic figure. Label the dimensions and find the total area.

6.4 Practice
For use after Lesson 6.4

Each square on the grid paper is 1 square inch. Find the area of the figure.

1.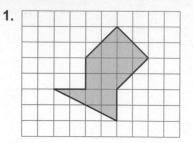

2.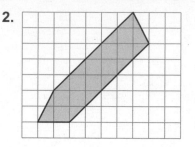

Find the area of the figure.

3.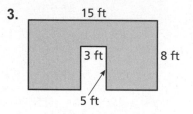

4.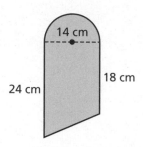

5. The diagram shows the shape of the green of a miniature golf hole. What is the area of the green?

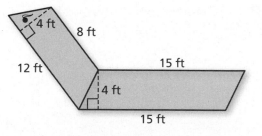

Name_____ Date_____

Evaluate the expression when $x = 3$ and $y = 5$.

1. $2xy$

2. $\dfrac{6y}{x}$

3. $4y - x$

4. $y^2 - 7x + 2$

Evaluate the expression when $x = \dfrac{1}{4}$ and $y = 8$.

5. $3xy$

6. $16x + 5y$

7. $\dfrac{y}{2x}$

8. $2(10 - 24x) + y^2$

9. After m months, you paid $25 + 10m$ for your computer. How much did you pay after 6 months?

Chapter 7 Fair Game Review (continued)

Write the phrase as an expression.

10. three more than twice a number k

11. half of a number q plus eight

12. a number p decreased by six

13. nine times a number x

14. five divided by a number n

15. one plus the product of a number y and three

16. Each classmate contributes $2 for charity. Write an expression for the amount of money raised by your class.

17. You save half of your paycheck plus an extra six dollars to buy a new bike. Write an expression for the amount of money you save of each paycheck.

7.1 **Writing Equations in One Variable**
For use with Activity 7.1

Essential Question How does rewriting a word problem help you solve the word problem?

1 **EXAMPLE:** Rewriting a Word Problem

Read the problem several times. Rewrite the problem. Leave out information you do not need to solve the problem.

Given Problem (63 words)

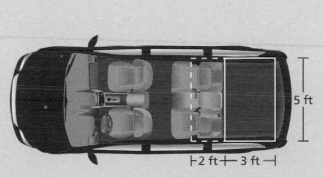

Your minivan has a flat, rectangular space in the back. When you fold down the rear seats of the van and move them forward, the rectangular space in the van is increased by 2 feet, as shown in the diagram.

By how many square feet does the area of the rectangular space increase when the rear seats are folded down and moved forward?

Rewritten Problem (29 words)

When you fold down the back seats of a minivan, the added space is a 5-foot by 2-foot rectangle. What is the area of the added space?

Can you make the problem even simpler?

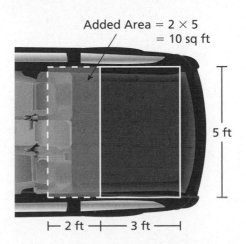

Added Area = 2×5
= 10 sq ft

Now the problem is easy to read. It asks you to find the area of the additional space after the back seats are folded down.

Name_____ Date _____

2 ACTIVITY: Rewriting a Word Problem

Work with a partner. Rewrite each problem until it is easy to read. Then solve the problem.

a. (62 words)

A supermarket is having its grand opening on Saturday morning. Every fifth customer will receive a $20 coupon for a free turkey. Every seventh customer will receive a $25 coupon for 2 gallons of free ice cream. You are the manager of the store and you expect 400 customers. How many of each type of coupon should you plan to use?

b. (72 words)

You and your friend are at a football game. The stadium is 4 miles from your home. You each brought 5 dollars to spend on refreshments. During the third quarter of the game, you say, "I read that the greatest distance that a baseball has been thrown is 445 feet 10 inches." Your friend says, "That's about one and a half times the length of the football field." Is your friend correct?

7.1 **Writing Equations in One Variable** (continued)

c. (90 words)

> You are visiting your cousin who lives in the city. To get back home, you take a taxi. The taxi charges $2.10 for the first mile and $0.90 for each additional mile. After riding 13 miles, you decide that the fare is going to be more than the $20 you have with you. So, you tell the driver to stop and let you out. Then you call a friend and ask your friend to come pick you up. After paying the driver, how much of your $20 is left?

What Is Your Answer?

3. **IN YOUR OWN WORDS** How does rewriting a word problem help you solve the word problem? Make up a word problem that has more than 50 words. Then show how you can rewrite the problem using at most 25 words.

"Solving a math word problem is like making maple syrup."

"You need to boil down 40 gallons of sap from a sugar maple tree to get 1 gallon of syrup."

7.1 Practice
For use after Lesson 7.1

Write the word sentence as an equation.

1. 27 is 3 times a number y.

2. The difference of a number x and 4 is 3.

3. 8 more than a number p is 17.

4. Half of a number q is 14.

Write an equation that can be used to find the value of x.

5. Perimeter of rectangle: 32 cm

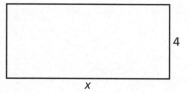

6. Perimeter of triangle: 20 in.

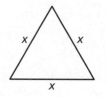

7. You spend $16 on 3 notebooks and x binders. Notebooks cost $2 each and binders cost $5 each. Write an equation you can use to find the number of binders you bought.

7.2 Solving Equations Using Addition or Subtraction
For use with Activity 7.2

Essential Question How can you use addition or subtraction to solve an equation?

If two sides of a scale weigh the same, the scale will balance.

If you add or subtract the same amount on each side of the scale, it will still balance.

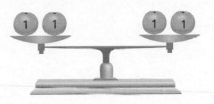

---

1 EXAMPLE: Solving an Equation Using Subtraction

Use a scale to model and solve $n + 3 = 7$.

Think of a scale with both sides in balance. Whatever you add to or subtract from one side, you need to do the same on the other side to keep the scale in balance.

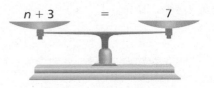

When $n + 3$ is on one side and 7 is on the other side, the scale is balanced.

Your goal is to get n by itself on one side. To do this, _____ from each side.

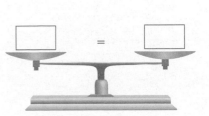

Simplify each side. The remaining value is the solution.

So, $n = $ _____.

7.2 **Solving Equations Using Addition or Subtraction** (continued)

2 **ACTIVITY:** Solving Equations Using Mental Math

Work with a partner. Write a question that represents the equation. Use mental math to answer the question. Then check your solution.

Equation	Question	Solution	Check
a. $x + 3 = 7$	What number plus 3 equals 7?	$x = 4$	$4 + 3 = 7$ ✓
b. $4 + m = 11$			
c. $8 = a + 3$			
d. $x - 9 = 21$			
e. $13 = p - 4$			

3 **ACTIVITY:** Solving Equations Using Addition or Subtraction

Work with a partner. Solve the equation using Example 1 as a sample.

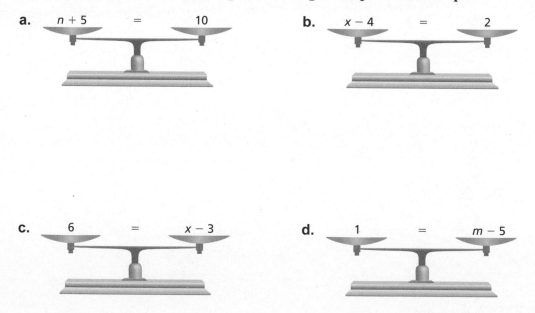

a. $n + 5 = 10$

b. $x - 4 = 2$

c. $6 = x - 3$

d. $1 = m - 5$

7.2 Solving Equations Using Addition or Subtraction (continued)

What Is Your Answer?

4. Decide whether the statement is *true* or *false*. If false, explain your reasoning.

   a. In an equation, any letter can be used as a variable.

   b. The goal in solving an equation is to get the variable by itself.

   c. In the solution, the variable must always be on the left side of the equal sign.

   d. If you add a number to one side, you should subtract it from the other side.

   e. If you add a number to one side, you should add it to the other side.

5. **IN YOUR OWN WORDS** How can you use addition or subtraction to solve an equation? Give two examples to show how your procedure works.

Name _____ Date _____

7.2 Practice
For use after Lesson 7.2

Tell whether the given value is a solution of the equation.

1. $34 + x = 46; x = 12$

2. $y - 9 = 14; y = 22$

3. $6d = 54; d = 9$

4. $\dfrac{n}{3} = 13; n = 39$

Solve the equation. Check your solution.

5. $7 + k = 11$

6. $p - 24 = 13$

7. $b - 16 = 7$

8. $\dfrac{2}{5} + m = \dfrac{5}{6}$

9. In the heavyweight class of professional wrestling, the junior weight limit is 190 pounds. This is 15 pounds heavier than the light heavyweight limit. Write and solve an equation to find the weight limit of the light heavyweight class.

7.3 Solving Equations Using Multiplication or Division
For use with Activity 7.3

Essential Question How can you use multiplication or division to solve an equation?

---

1 ACTIVITY: Writing and Solving Multiplication Equations

Work with a partner. Solve for x. Check your answer.

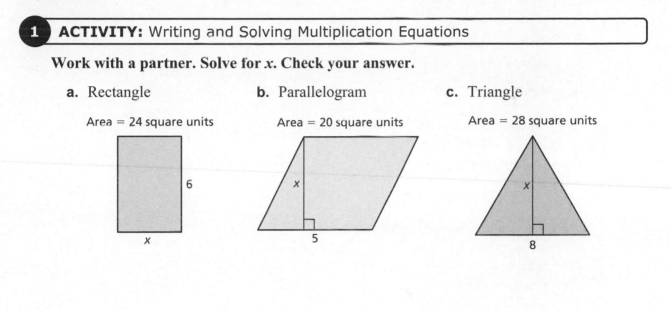

a. Rectangle

Area = 24 square units

6

x

b. Parallelogram

Area = 20 square units

x

5

c. Triangle

Area = 28 square units

x

8

---

2 EXAMPLE: Using an Equation to Model a Story

The problem is represented by the equation.

Problem	Equation
Three people go to lunch. They decide to share the $12 bill evenly. How much does each person pay?	$3x = 12$

• **What does x represent?**

• **Solve for x.**

• **Answer the question.**

So, each person pays _____.

7.3 Solving Equations Using Multiplication or Division (continued)

3 **ACTIVITY:** Using Equations to Model a Story

Work with a partner. Each problem is represented by the equation.

- What does x represent?
- Solve for x.
- Answer the question.

Problem	Equation
a. Three robots go out to lunch. They decide to share the $11.91 bill evenly. How much does each robot pay?	$3x = 11.91$
b. On Earth, objects weigh 6 times what they weigh on the moon. A robot weighs 96 pounds on Earth. What does it weigh on the moon?	$6x = 96$
c. At maximum speed, a robot runs 6 feet in 1 second. How many feet does the robot run in 1 minute?	$\dfrac{x}{60} = 6$
d. Four identical robots lie on the ground head-to-toe and measure 14 feet. How tall is each robot?	$4x = 14$

7.3 **Solving Equations Using Multiplication or Division** (continued)

What Is Your Answer?

4. Complete each sentence by matching.

- The inverse operation of addition
- The inverse operation of subtraction
- The inverse operation of multiplication
- The inverse operation of division

- is multiplication.
- is subtraction.
- is addition.
- is division.

5. IN YOUR OWN WORDS How can you use multiplication or division to solve an equation? Give two examples to show how your procedure works.

7.3 Practice
For use after Lesson 7.3

Solve the equation. Check your solution.

1. $7k = 77$

2. $\dfrac{p}{5} = 10$

3. $3 = \dfrac{m}{12}$

4. $4a = 36$

5. $5 \bullet x = 12$

6. $4.2 = \dfrac{c}{8}$

7. You earn $5 for every friendship bracelet you sell. Write and solve an equation to find the number of bracelets you have to sell to earn $85.

8. You practice the piano for 30 minutes each day. Write and solve an equation to find the total time t you spend practicing the piano for a week.

7.4 Solving Two-Step Equations
For use with Activity 7.4

Essential Question What is a "two-step" equation? How can you solve a two-step equation?

Sir Isaac Newton's Third Law of Motion

For every action, there is an equal and opposite reaction.

A teddy bear
Sits in a chair.
Down pushes Teddy.

Chair says "I'm ready."
With a confident "Yup"
The chair pushes up.

Because $5 - 5 = 0$, neither the bear nor the chair moves.

1 ACTIVITY: Identifying Inverse Operations

Work with a partner. Describe how you can "undo" the operation in bold.

a. $3x + 5 = 14$

b. $2n - 6 = 4$

c. $2(m + 3) = 6$

d. $\dfrac{x - 2}{4} = 1$

7.4 Solving Two-Step Equations (continued)

2 **ACTIVITY:** Solving Two-Step Equations

Work with a partner. Solve each equation in Activity 1. Use substitution to check your answer.

    a. $3x + 5 = 14$ **b.** $2n - 6 = 4$

    c. $2(m + 3) = 6$ **d.** $(x - 2) \div 4 = 1$

3 **ACTIVITY:** Analyzing a Video Game

Work with a partner. For Level 1 in a video game, you have to accomplish a sequence of challenges. Then, you have to leave the level by undoing the challenges in reverse order.

7.4   **Solving Two-Step Equations** (continued)

    a.   Describe the challenges in the video game in order.

    b.   Describe the order of challenges to get out of the level.

    c.   The screen shows Level 1 of the video game. Make up challenges for Level 2. Draw the level and describe the reverse order to get back out of the level.

What Is Your Answer?

    4. IN YOUR OWN WORDS What is a "two-step" equation? How can you solve a two-step equation? Give an example to show how your procedure works.

"Hey, it says 'Close this flap first,'
but they closed it last!"

Name _____ Date _____

7.4 Practice
For use after Lesson 7.4

Solve the equation. Check your solution.

1. $4k + 2 = 6$

2. $\dfrac{p}{6} - 9 = 3$

3. $21 = \dfrac{r}{3} + 3$

4. $\dfrac{a}{5} - 8 = 1$

5. $7x + 9 = 51$

6. $37 = 6g - 11$

7. $2x + x = 33$

8. $49 = 10p - 3p$

9. $42.3 = 1.5d + 3.2d$

10. You need to save $5 more than 8 times your paycheck to buy a dirt bike. Your paycheck is $50. How much money do you need to save?

11. You sell tickets for a fundraiser. You give half of the tickets to your sister to sell. You sell 25 of your half of the tickets and have 17 left. How many tickets did you start with?

7.5 Finding Dimensions of Plane Figures
For use with Activity 7.5

Essential Question How can you use area and perimeter formulas to find missing dimensions of plane figures?

1 ACTIVITY: Finding Missing Dimensions

Work with a partner. Match the equation with a figure. Then use the equation to solve for *x*.

a. Area: $24 = 4x$

b. Perimeter: $24 = 4x$

c. Circumference: $8\pi = 2\pi x$

d. Area: $20 = 5x$

e. Area: $16 = \dfrac{1}{2}x(5 + 3)$

f. Area: $10 = \dfrac{1}{2}(5x)$

g. Perimeter: $30 = 20 + 2x$

h. Circumference: $4\pi = \pi x$

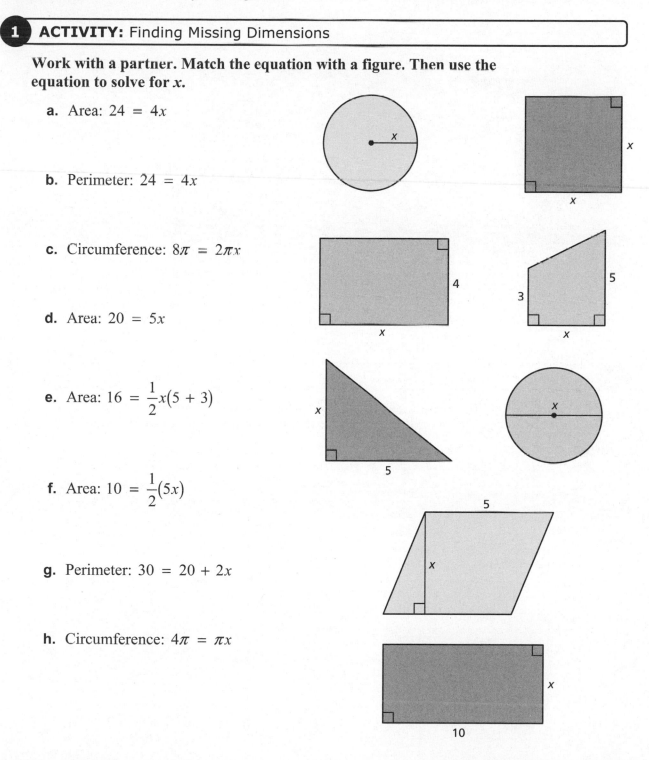

7.5 **Finding Dimensions of Plane Figures** (continued)

2 **ACTIVITY:** Finding Dimensions

Work with a partner. This is a sign at Madeira Beach Fundamental School.
Estimate the missing dimension.

83 inches

x

3 **ACTIVITY:** Drawing a School Logo

Work with a partner. Draw your school's logo on grid paper. Assign a scale
to your drawing. Estimate the area and perimeter of all or part of your logo.

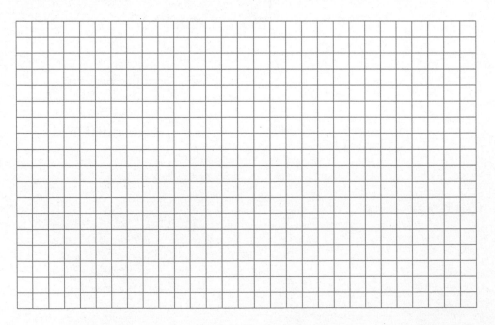

7.5 Finding Dimensions of Plane Figures (continued)

What Is Your Answer?

4. **IN YOUR OWN WORDS** How can you use area and perimeter formulas to find missing dimensions of plane figures? Draw a plane figure and label its dimensions. Find the area or perimeter. Then erase one of the dimensions and show how you can use algebra to find it again.

7.5 **Practice**
For use after Lesson 7.5

**Write and solve an equation to find the missing dimension of the figure.
Check your solution.**

1. Perimeter = 44 in.

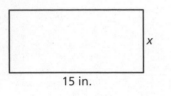

15 in.

x

2. Area = 48 m²

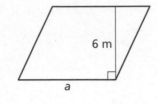

6 m

a

3. Circumference = 9π ft

r

4. Area = 144 mm²

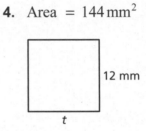

12 mm

t

5. The area of the face of a basketball backboard is 21 square feet. What is the width?

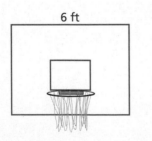

6 ft

6. The area of the infield of a track is 10,335 square meters. Find x. Round your answer to the nearest tenth.

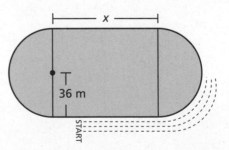

x

36 m

START

Name_____ Date_____

Essential Question How can you use a volume formula to find missing dimensions of prisms?

1 **ACTIVITY:** Finding Missing Dimensions

Work with a partner. Solve the equation for x.

a. Volume: $264 = 24x$

8 in.   3 in. x

b. Volume: $162 = 18x$

4.5 in.   4 in. x

c. Volume: $45 = 9x$

6 in.   1.5 in. x

d. Volume: $12 = 8x$

4 in.   2 in. x

7.6 **Finding Dimensions of Prisms** (continued)

e. Volume: $288 = 48x$

12 in.　　　　　　　　*x*　　4 in.

ACTIVITY: Finding Dimensions

Work with a partner. Is there enough information given to estimate the volume of each building? If not, explain why. If there is enough information, estimate the volume of the building.

Republic Plaza
Denver, CO
56 Stories: 714 ft
1,340,000 ft^2 floor space

Seagram Building
New York, NY
38 Stories: 515 ft
820,000 ft^2 floor space

Espirito Santo Plaza
Miami, FL
37 Stories: 483 ft
750,000 ft^2 floor space

7.6 **Finding Dimensions of Prisms** (continued)

What Is Your Answer?

3. **IN YOUR OWN WORDS** How can you use a volume formula to find missing dimensions of prisms?

4. Design a skyscraper that will be 10% taller than one of the skyscrapers in Activity 2. Find its volume.

"Dear Sir. The question
'How much is half of 8?'
is confusing."

"If you mean up and down, the
answer is 3. If you mean sideways,
the answer is 0."

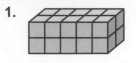 **Practice**
For use after Lesson 7.6

Find the number of cubes it takes to fill the box.

1.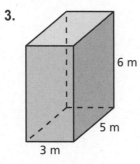

2.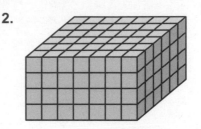

Find the volume of the rectangular prism.

3.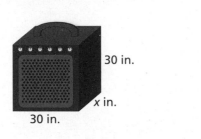

4.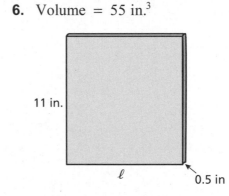

Write and solve an equation to find the missing dimension of the rectangular prism.

5. Volume = 18,000 in.^{3}

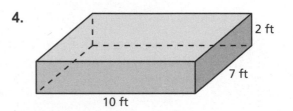

30 in.

x in.

30 in.

6. Volume = 55 in.^{3}

11 in.

ℓ

0.5 in

7. You are mailing a birthday present to a friend. You have a box that has a length of 3 feet, a height of 2 feet, and a width of 2 feet.

a. If the present has a volume of 3 cubic feet, what is the volume of the empty space in the box?

b. You can buy 1.5 cubic feet of packing peanuts in each bag. About how many bags of packing peanuts do you need to buy to fill the box?

 **Practice**
For use after Lesson 7.6b

Use cubes with the given edge length to find the volume of the rectangular prism. Check your answer using the volume formula.

1. Edge length: $\dfrac{1}{2}$ ft

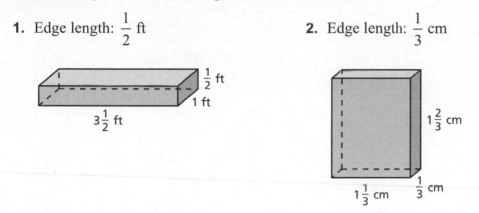

$\dfrac{1}{2}$ ft

1 ft

$3\dfrac{1}{2}$ ft

2. Edge length: $\dfrac{1}{3}$ cm

$1\dfrac{2}{3}$ cm

$1\dfrac{1}{3}$ cm

$\dfrac{1}{3}$ cm

Find the surface area of the rectangular prism.

3.

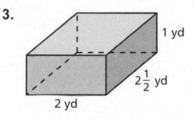

1 yd

$2\dfrac{1}{2}$ yd

2 yd

4.

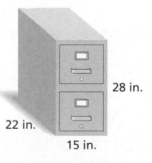

28 in.

22 in.

15 in.

Name _____ Date _____

7.6b **Practice** (continued)

Find the surface area of the triangular prism.

5.

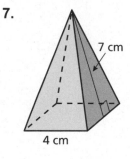

13 m

5 m

12 m

7 m

6.

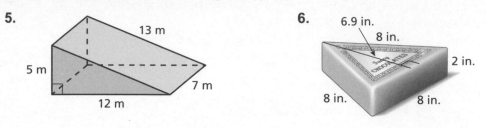

6.9 in.

8 in.

2 in.

8 in.

8 in.

Find the surface area of the square pyramid.

7.

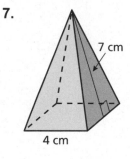

7 cm

4 cm

8.

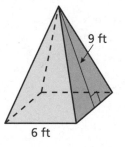

9 ft

6 ft

170B **Big Ideas Math Green**
Record and Practice Journal

Name_____ Date_____

Chapter 8 **Fair Game Review**

Use a number line to order the numbers from least to greatest.

1. $\dfrac{2}{3}, \dfrac{5}{6}, \dfrac{1}{2}, 1$

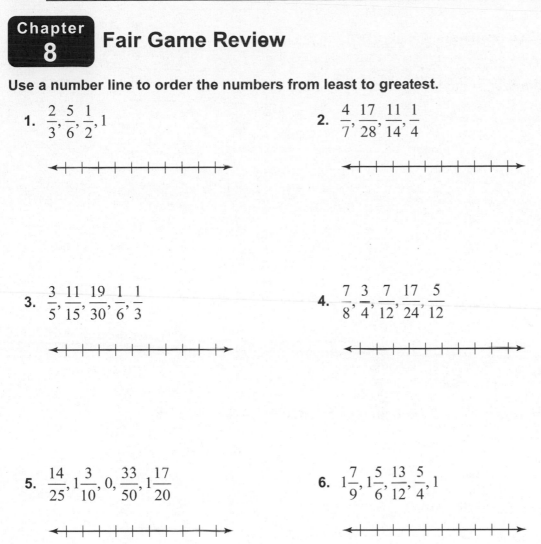

2. $\dfrac{4}{7}, \dfrac{17}{28}, \dfrac{11}{14}, \dfrac{1}{4}$

3. $\dfrac{3}{5}, \dfrac{11}{15}, \dfrac{19}{30}, \dfrac{1}{6}, \dfrac{1}{3}$

4. $\dfrac{7}{8}, \dfrac{3}{4}, \dfrac{7}{12}, \dfrac{17}{24}, \dfrac{5}{12}$

5. $\dfrac{14}{25}, 1\dfrac{3}{10}, 0, \dfrac{33}{50}, 1\dfrac{17}{20}$

6. $1\dfrac{7}{9}, 1\dfrac{5}{6}, \dfrac{13}{12}, \dfrac{5}{4}, 1$

7. The table shows wrench sizes. Order the wrench sizes from least to greatest.

Wrench	Size
A	$\dfrac{5}{32}$
B	$\dfrac{1}{4}$
C	$\dfrac{3}{16}$
D	$\dfrac{9}{32}$

Copyright © Big Ideas Learning, LLC
All rights reserved.

Big Ideas Math Green **171**
Record and Practice Journal

Chapter 8 **Fair Game Review** (continued)

Complete the number sentence with <, >, or =.

8. 5 ___ 8

9. 13 ___ 9

10. 0.3 ___ $\dfrac{3}{8}$

11. 0.68 ___ $\dfrac{17}{25}$

12. 3.6 ___ $\dfrac{12}{5}$

13. 0.06 ___ 0.062

Find three numbers that make the number sentence true.

14. 0.35 < ___

15. $\dfrac{4}{9}$ ≥ ___

16. $2\dfrac{3}{5}$ ≤ ___

17. $\dfrac{1}{10}$ < ___

18. 0.485 ≥ ___

19. 5.87 ≤ ___

20. During a trivia game, you answered 18 out of 25 questions correctly. Your friend answered 0.7 of the questions correctly. Write a number sentence for who had the greater number of correct answers.

8.1 Writing and Graphing Inequalities
For use with Activity 8.1

Essential Question How can you use a number line to represent solutions of an inequality?

1 ACTIVITY: Understanding Inequality Statements

Work with a partner.

a. Consider the statement "Your friend is *more than* 3 minutes late."

- Circle each number that makes the statement true.

    −3   −2   −1   0   1   2   3   4   5   6

- Write four other numbers that make the statement true.

b. Consider the statement "The temperature is *at most* 2 degrees."

- Can the temperature be exactly 2 degrees? Explain.

- Circle each number that makes the statement true.

    −5   −4   −3   −2   −1   0   1   2   3   4

- Write four other numbers that make the statement true.

c. Consider the statement "You need *at least* 4 pieces of paper for your math homework."

- Can you have exactly 4 pieces of paper? Explain.

- Circle each number that makes the statement true.

    −3   −2   −1   0   1   2   3   4   5   6

- Write four other numbers that make the statement true.

3.1 **Writing and Graphing Inequalities** (continued)

d. Consider the statement "After playing a video game for 20 minutes, you have *fewer than* 6 points."

- Circle each number that makes the statement true.

  −2   −1   0   1   2   3   4   5   6   7

- Write four other numbers that make the statement true.

ACTIVITY: Understanding Inequality Symbols

Work with a partner.

a. Consider the statement "*x* is a number such that $x < 2$."

- Can the number be exactly 2? Explain.

- Circle each number that makes the statement true.

  −5   −4   −3   −2   −1   0   1   2   3   4

- Write four other numbers that make the statement true.

b. Consider the statement "*x* is a number such that $x \geq 1$."

- Can the number be exactly 1? Explain.

- Circle each number that makes the statement true.

  −5   −4   −3   −2   −1   0   1   2   3   4

- Write four other numbers that make the statement true.

8.1 **Writing and Graphing Inequalities** (continued)

3 **ACTIVITY:** How Close Can You Come to 0?

Work with a partner.

a. Which number line shows $x > 0$? Which number line shows $x \geq 0$?
Explain your reasoning.

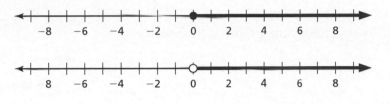

b. Write the least positive number you can think of that is still a
solution of the inequality $x > 0$. Explain your reasoning.

What Is Your Answer?

4. IN YOUR OWN WORDS How can you use a number line to represent
solutions of an inequality?

5. Write an inequality. Graph all solutions of your inequality on a
number line.

Name _____ Date _____

8.1 Practice
For use after Lesson 8.1

Write the word sentence as an inequality.

1. A number n is at least 4.

2. A number x is less than 12.

Tell whether the given value is a solution of the inequality.

3. $4x \leq 20$; $x = 2$

4. $y + 5 > 8$; $y = 1$

Graph the inequality on a number line.

5. $x < 5$

6. $w \geq -\dfrac{1}{4}$

7. You buy tickets to a professional football game. You are allowed to buy at most 4 tickets. Each ticket is no less than $65.

   a. Write and graph an inequality to represent the number of tickets you are allowed to buy.

   b. Write and graph an inequality to represent the cost of each ticket you are allowed to buy.

8.2 Solving Inequalities Using Addition or Subtraction
For use with Activity 8.2

Essential Question How can you use an inequality to describe a real-life situation?

---

1 **ACTIVITY:** Writing an Inequality

Work with a partner. In 3 years, your friend will still not be old enough to apply for a driver's license.

    a. Which of the following represents your friend's situation? What does x represent? Explain your reasoning.

$x + 3 < 16$	$x + 3 \leq 16$	$x + 3 > 16$	$x + 3 \geq 16$

    b. Graph the possible ages of your friend on a number line.

---

2 **ACTIVITY:** The Triangle Inequality

Work with a partner. Draw different triangles whose sides have lengths 10 cm, 6 cm, and x cm.

    a. Which of the following describes how *small* x can be?

$6 + x < 10$	$6 + x \leq 10$

$6 + x > 10$	$6 + x \geq 10$

    b. Which of the following describes how *large* x can be?

$x - 6 < 10$	$x - 6 \leq 10$

$x - 6 > 10$	$x - 6 \geq 10$

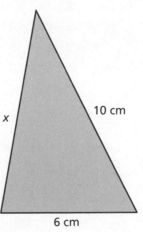

8.2 **Solving Inequalities Using Addition or Subtraction** (continued)

3 ACTIVITY: Writing an Inequality

Work with a partner. Baby manatees are about 4 feet long at birth. They grow to a maximum length of 13 feet.

   a. Which of the following can represent a baby manatee's growth? What does x represent? Explain your reasoning.

| $x + 4 < 13$ | $x + 4 \leq 13$ | $x - 4 > 13$ | $x - 4 \geq 13$ |

   b. Graph the solution on a number line.

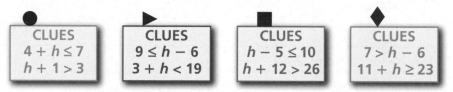

4 ACTIVITY: Puzzles

Work with a partner.

   a. Use the clues to find the word that is spelled by ●, ▶, ■, ♦. Assume $A = 1$, $B = 2$, and so on.

●	▶	■	♦
CLUES	**CLUES**	**CLUES**	**CLUES**
$4 + h \leq 7$	$9 \leq h - 6$	$h - 5 \leq 10$	$7 > h - 6$
$h + 1 > 3$	$3 + h < 19$	$h + 12 > 26$	$11 + h \geq 23$

   b. Use the cut-out pieces. Rearrange them to make a square without overlapping the pieces.*

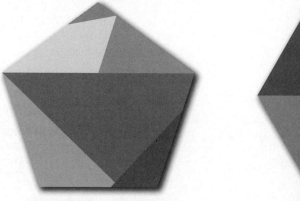

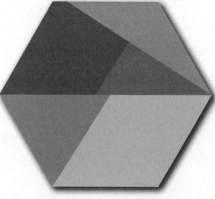

            Pentagon to Square   Hexagon to Square

*Cut-outs are available in the back of the Record and Practice Journal.

Name_____ Date _____

8.2 **Solving Inequalities Using Addition or Subtraction** (continued)

c. Use exactly four 4's and the operations +, −, ×, and ÷ to write expressions
that have values of 0, 1, 2, 3, 4, 5, 6, 7, 8, 9, and 10. For instance 44 − 44 = 0.

What Is Your Answer?

5. IN YOUR OWN WORDS How can you use an inequality to describe
a real-life situation?

6. Write a real-life situation that you can represent with an inequality.
Write the inequality. Graph the solution on a number line.

Name_____ Date _____

Solve the inequality. Graph the solution.

1. $x + 6 \leq 15$

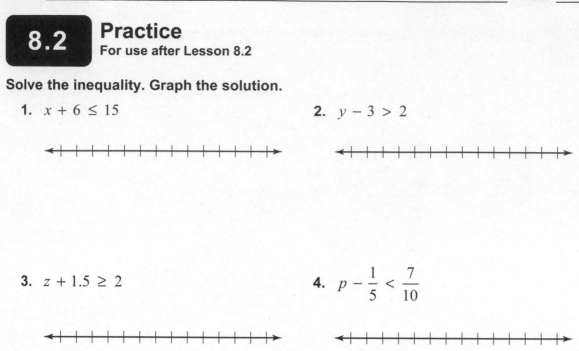

2. $y - 3 > 2$

3. $z + 1.5 \geq 2$

4. $p - \dfrac{1}{5} < \dfrac{7}{10}$

5. Your teacher gives you an assignment and says you have at most 2 weeks to complete the assignment. You are still working on the assignment after 5 days. Write and solve an inequality to represent how much more time you have to meet the requirement.

6. You are taking a history course in which your grade is based on six 100-point tests. To earn an A in the class, you must have a total of at least 90%. You have scored an 83, 89, 95, 98, and 92 on the first five tests. What is the least amount of points you can earn on the sixth test in order to earn an A in the course?

8.3 Solving Inequalities Using Multiplication or Division
For use with Activity 8.3

Essential Question How can you use multiplication or division to solve an inequality?

1 ACTIVITY: Matching Inequalities

Work with a partner. Match the inequality with its graph.

a. $3x < 9$ b. $3x \leq 9$ c. $\dfrac{x}{2} \geq 1$

d. $6 < 2x$ e. $12 \leq 4x$ f. $\dfrac{x}{2} < 2$

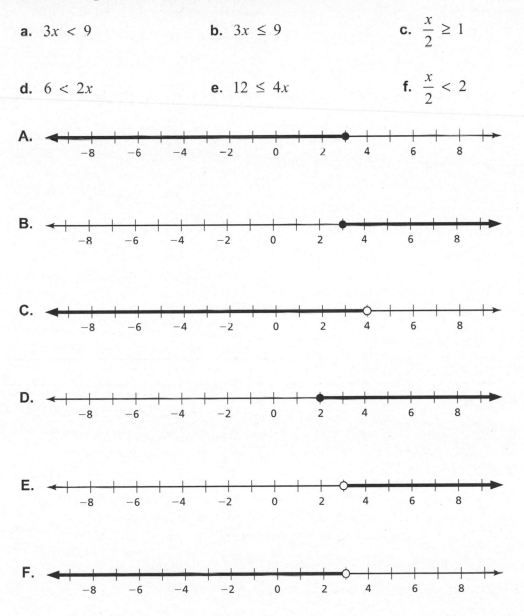

8.3 **Solving Inequalities Using Multiplication or Division** (continued)

2 **ACTIVITY:** Writing an Inequality

Work with a partner. One of your favorite stores is having a 75% off sale. You have $20. You want to buy a pair of jeans.

  a. Which of the following represents your ability to buy the jeans with $20?

| $0.25x < 20$ | $0.25x \leq 20$ | $0.25x > 20$ | $0.25x \geq 20$ |

  b. What does x represent? Graph the possible values of x on a number line.

  c. Can you afford a pair of jeans that originally costs $100? Explain.

3 **ACTIVITY:** Spaceman Game

Play with a partner.

  • Player 1: Start the game by choosing an inequality from the list on the next page that has a solution of $x \geq 1$. This allows you to destroy Asteroids 1, 2, and 3.

  • Player 2: Asteroid 3 is destroyed. Choose an inequality from the list on the next page that has a solution of $x > 3$ or $x \geq 4$. This allows you to destroy Asteroid 4, an alien, and Asteroid 6.

  • You can only destroy asteroids and aliens in a straight line.

  • Each asteroid is worth 1 point. Each alien is worth 2 points.

  • Take turns until someone reaches the end of the maze. The player with the most points wins.

  • If an incorrect inequality is chosen, then the player loses that turn.

Name_____ Date _____

$x + 13 \geq 90$

$x - 2 \geq 5$

$39 < 3x$

$65 < x + 10$

$2x \geq 22$

$x + 5 > 24$

$33 \leq x - 5$

$3x > 126$

$6 < x - 2$

$x + 2 \geq 3$

$x + 30 \geq 84$

$35 \leq x + 6$

$32 \leq x - 29$

$7x > 441$

$110 < x + 32$

$180 \leq 4x$

$x - 52 \geq 32$

$x - 9 > 21$

$2x \geq 178$

$4 < x + 1$

$x - 24 > 34$

$58 < x - 28$

$134 < 2x$

$\dfrac{x}{2} \geq 45$

$17 < \dfrac{x}{3}$

$\dfrac{x}{3} \geq 5$

$8 \leq \dfrac{x}{2}$

$\dfrac{x}{4} \geq 12$

$\dfrac{x}{5} > 14$

$37 \leq \dfrac{x}{2}$

What Is Your Answer?

4. **IN YOUR OWN WORDS** How can you use multiplication and division to solve an inequality?

8.3 Practice
For use after Lesson 8.3

Solve the inequality. Graph the solution.

1. $12q \geq 36$

2. $\dfrac{t}{4} > 6$

Graph the numbers that are solutions to both inequalities.

3. $6a \leq 42$ and $a + 4 > 7$

4. $d - 8 \leq 2$ and $9d < 81$

5. Each table in a banquet room seats 8 people. The room can seat no more than 360 people. Write and solve an inequality to represent the number of tables in the banquet room.

6. To play a board game, there must be at least 4 people on each team. You divide your friends into 3 groups. Write and solve an inequality to represent the number of friends playing the game.

8.4 Solving Two-Step Inequalities
For use with Activity 8.4

Essential Question How can you use inequalities to classify different species of animals?

1 ACTIVITY: Classifying Dinosaurs

Work with a partner. Let *L* represent the length of an adult dinosaur.

a. Put each species of dinosaur shown on the following pages into the correct region in the diagram.

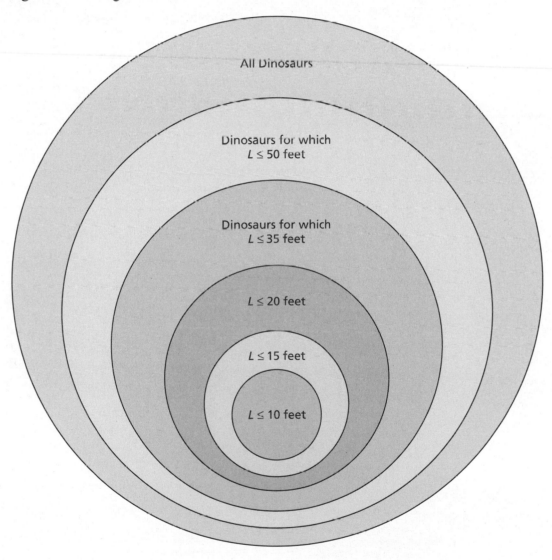

All Dinosaurs

Dinosaurs for which
$L \le 50$ feet

Dinosaurs for which
$L \le 35$ feet

$L \le 20$ feet

$L \le 15$ feet

$L \le 10$ feet

8.4 Solving Two-Step Inequalities (continued)

Tyrannosaurus Rex
About 40 feet long and 7 tons
Pronounced tih-RAN-oh-SORE-us REX

Spinosaurus
About 50 feet long and 7 tons
Pronounced SPINE-oh-SORE-us

Camarasaurus
About 60 feet long and 20 tons
Pronounced cam-AH-rah-SORE-us

Plateosaurus
About 25 feet long and 2 tons
Pronounced PLAT-ee-oh-SORE-us

Protoceratops
About 6 feet long and 400 pounds
Pronounced PRO-toe-SER-ah-tops

8.4   **Solving Two-Step Inequalities** (continued)

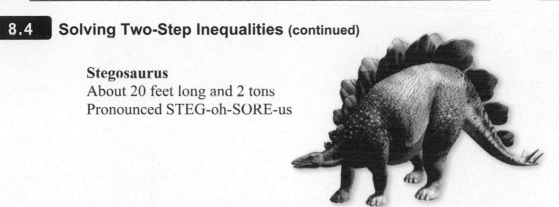

Stegosaurus
About 20 feet long and 2 tons
Pronounced STEG-oh-SORE-us

b. Are all the dinosaur species that are in the "$L \leq 35$ feet" category also in the "$L \leq 50$ feet" category? Explain your reasoning.

c. Are all the dinosaur species that are in the "$L \leq 35$ feet" category also in the "$L \leq 20$ feet" category? Explain your reasoning.

d. Draw a different diagram that classifies the six dinosaur species by weight.

What Is Your Answer?

2. IN YOUR OWN WORDS How can you use inequalities to classify different species of animals?

3. RESEARCH Find two other species of dinosaur that you can include in the two diagrams.

8.4 Practice
For use after Lesson 8.4

Solve the inequality. Graph the solution.

1. $3n - 6 < 12$

2. $\dfrac{a}{5} + 8 \geq 27$

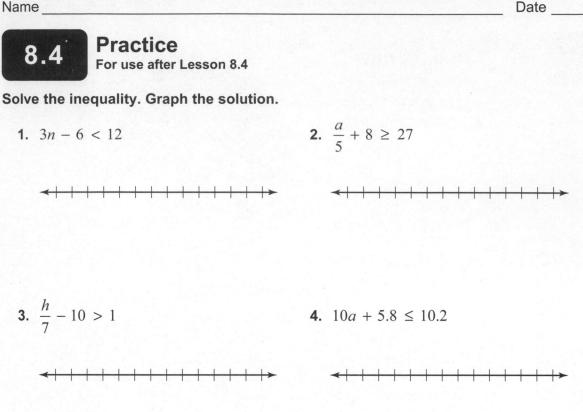

3. $\dfrac{h}{7} - 10 > 1$

4. $10a + 5.8 \leq 10.2$

The area of the figure is at least 200 square feet. Write and solve a two-step inequality to represent the possible values of *x*. Use 3.14 for π.

5.

10 ft

17 ft

x

6.

16 ft

x

7. You budget $50 a month for your cell phone plan. You pay $45 for your minutes and 250 text messages. You are charged an extra $0.50 for picture messages. Write and solve an inequality to find the number of picture messages you can send without going over your budget.

Name_____ Date _____

Fair Game Review

Using the numbers from the In and Out Table, find and state the rule in words.

1.

In	Out
1	4
2	5
3	6
4	7

2.

In	Out
2	6
4	12
6	18
8	24

3.

In	Out
12	2
24	14
36	26
48	38

4.

In	Out
4	2
5	$\frac{5}{2}$
6	3
7	$\frac{7}{2}$

5. The In and Out Table shows the results of buying pretzels from a vending machine. The in column is the amount you put into the machine. The out column is the change you receive back from the machine. Complete the table and state the rule in words.

In	Out
0.65	0
0.70	0.05
0.75	0.10
1.00	

Chapter 9

Fair Game Review (continued)

Use the graph to write an ordered pair corresponding to the point.

6. Point *A*

7. Point *B*

8. Point *C*

9. Point *D*

10. Point *E*

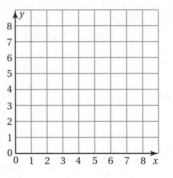

Plot the point on the graph.

11. $P(2, 5)$

12. $Q(0, 1)$

13. $R(3, 3)$

14. $S(4, 2)$

15. $T(5, 0)$

9.1 Mapping Diagrams
For use with Activity 9.1

Essential Question What is a mapping diagram? How can it be used to represent a function?

1 **ACTIVITY:** Constructing Mapping Diagrams

Work with a partner. Complete the mapping diagram.

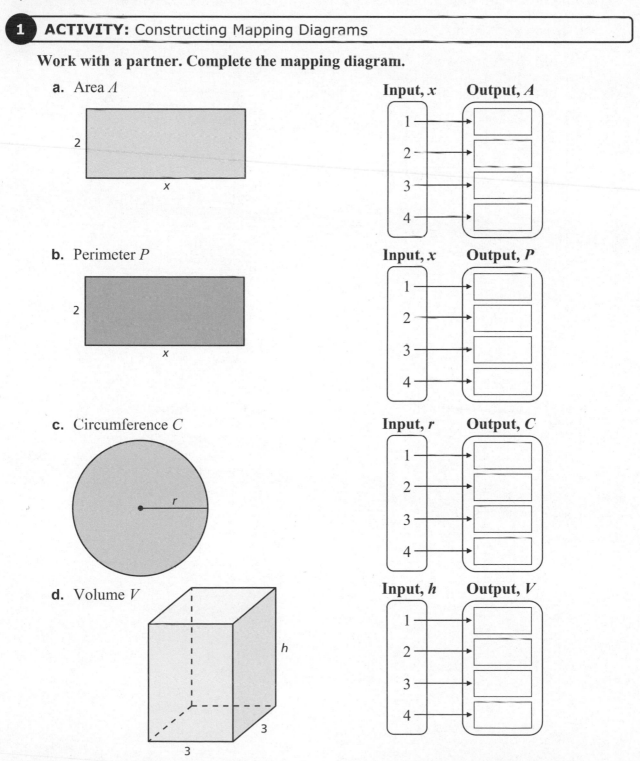

a. Area A

2

x

Input, x Output, A

1
2
3
4

b. Perimeter P

2

x

Input, x Output, P

1
2
3
4

c. Circumference C

r

Input, r Output, C

1
2
3
4

d. Volume V

h

3

3

Input, h Output, V

1
2
3
4

9.1 Mapping Diagrams (continued)

2 **ACTIVITY:** Interpreting Mapping Diagrams

Work with a partner. Describe the pattern in the mapping diagram. Complete the diagram. Find two earlier lessons where you used a similar function.

a. Input, d Output, P

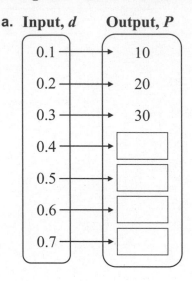

b. Input, t Output, M

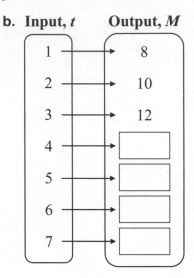

c. Input, n Output, S

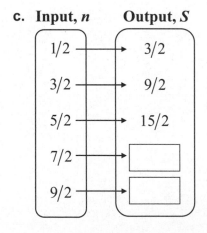

d. Input, x Output, A

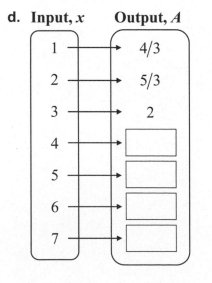

What Is Your Answer?

3. **IN YOUR OWN WORDS** What is a mapping diagram? How can it be used to represent a function?

4. Construct a mapping diagram that represents a function you have studied.

"I made a mapping diagram."

"It shows how I feel about my skateboard with each passing day."

Name _____ Date _____

List the ordered pairs shown in the mapping diagram.

1. Input   Output

    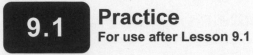

2. Input   Output

Draw a mapping diagram of the set of ordered pairs.

3. $(1, 7), (3, 4), (4, 8), (7, 2)$

4. $(0, 3), (2, 4), (5, 4), (8, 5)$

5. Draw a mapping diagram for the graph. Then describe the pattern of inputs and outputs.

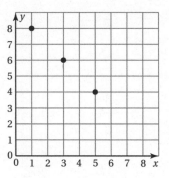

6. The table shows the number of beads needed to make a bracelet. Use the table to draw a mapping diagram.

Bracelet Length (in.)	Number of Beads
6	12
7	14
8	16
9	18

Name_____ Date_____

9.2 Functions as Words and Equations
For use with Activity 9.2

Essential Question How can you describe a function with words? How can you describe a function with an equation?

1 ACTIVITY: Describing a Function

Work with a partner. Two mapping diagrams related to the rectangle are shown. Describe each function in words. Then write an equation for each function.

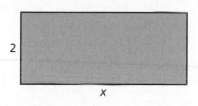

a. Area *A*

    Input, *x*   **Output, *A***

| 1 → 2 |
| 2 → 4 |
| 3 → 6 |
| 4 → 8 |

b. Perimeter *P*

    Input, *x*   **Output, *P***

| 1 → 6 |
| 2 → 8 |
| 3 → 10 |
| 4 → 12 |

2 ACTIVITY: Describing a Function

Work with a partner. Complete the mapping diagram on the next page for the area of the figure. Then write an equation that describes the function.

a.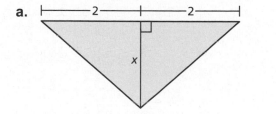

b.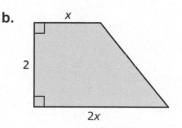

9.2 **Functions as Words and Equations** (continued)

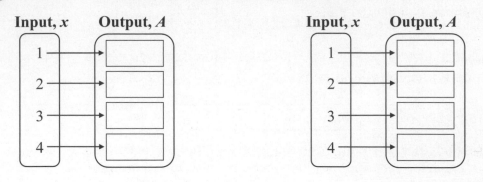

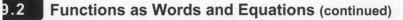

ACTIVITY: Describing a Function

Work with a partner. Complete the mapping diagram. Then write an equation that describes the function.

a. Sales tax of 6%

Input, x	Output, T
Cost ($)	Sales Tax ($)

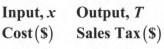

b. Phone bill of $5 per hour

Input, x	Output, B
Hours	Bill ($)

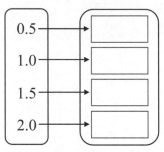

c. Perimeter of a square

Input, s	Output, P
Side (in.)	Perimeter (in.)

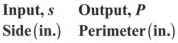
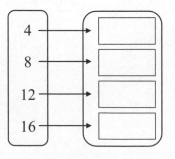

d. Surface area of a cube

Input, s	Output, S
Side (m)	Surface Area (m^2)

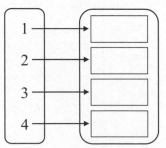

Name_____ Date_____

e. Circumference of a circle

Input, r   **Output, C**
Radius (ft) **Circumference (in.)**

```
4  ─────▶ ┌──────────┐
         │          │
8  ─────▶ ├──────────┤
         │          │
12 ─────▶ ├──────────┤
         │          │
16 ─────▶ └──────────┘
```

f. Area of a semicircle

Input, r   **Output, A**
Radius (cm) **Area (cm²)**

```
1  ─────▶ ┌──────────┐
         │          │
2  ─────▶ ├──────────┤
         │          │
3  ─────▶ ├──────────┤
         │          │
4  ─────▶ └──────────┘
```

What Is Your Answer?

4. IN YOUR OWN WORDS How can you describe a function with words? How can you describe a function with an equation? Give some examples from lessons you have studied this year.

9.2 Practice
For use after Lesson 9.2

Write an equation that describes the function.

1. The output is four times the input.

2. The output is eight less than the input.

Find the value of *y* for the given value of *x*.

3. $y = \dfrac{x}{3}; x = 12$

4. $y = 5x + 9; x = 2$

Tell whether the ordered pair is a solution of the equation.

5. $y = 6x - 7; (2, 5)$

6. $y = \dfrac{x}{2} + 1; (3, 4)$

7. You set up a hot chocolate stand at a football game. The cost of your supplies is $75. You charge $0.50 for each cup of hot chocolate.

    a. Write an equation you can use to find the profit *P* for selling *c* cups of hot chocolate.

    b. You will *break even* if the cost of your supplies equals your income. How many cups of hot chocolate must you sell to break even?

Name_____ Date_____

Essential Question How can you use a table to describe a function?

1 ACTIVITY: Using a Function Table

Work with a partner.

a. Complete the table for the perimeter
of the rectangle.

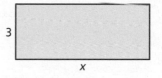

3

x

Input, x	1	2	3	4	5
Output, P					

b. Write an equation that describes the function.

c. Use your equation to find the values of x for which the perimeter is 50.

9.3 Input-Output Tables (continued)

2 ACTIVITY: Using a Function Table

Work with a partner. Use the strategy shown in Activity 1 to make a table that shows the pattern for the area. Write an equation that describes the function. Then use your equation to find which figure has an area of 81.

1 square unit

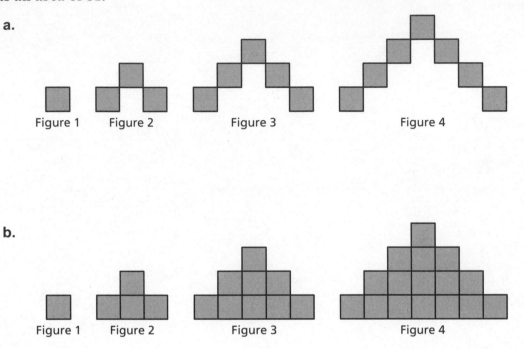

a.

Figure 1   Figure 2   Figure 3   Figure 4

b.

Figure 1   Figure 2   Figure 3   Figure 4

3 ACTIVITY: Making a Function Table

Work with a partner. Complete a sales tax table for each of the four cities.

Madison, WI, 5.50%

Sale, x	$20	$30	$40	$50	$60
Sales tax, T					

Ann Arbor, MI, 6.00%

Sale, x	$20	$30	$40	$50	$60
Sales tax, T					

9.3 **Input-Output Tables** (continued)

Edison, NJ, 7.00%

Sale, x	$20	$30	$40	$50	$60
Sales tax, T					

Norman, OK, 7.50%

Sale, x	$20	$30	$40	$50	$60
Sales tax, T					

What Is Your Answer?

4. **IN YOUR OWN WORDS** How can you use a table to describe a function?
   Describe an example of a function table in real life.

Amount of Sale	Tax
.10 - .16	.01
.17 - .33	.02
.34 - .50	.03
.51 - .66	.04
.67 - .83	.05
.84 - 1.09	.06

"Dear Slr: Yesterday, I bought a piece of 9-cent candy six times and paid NO tax. Today, I bought six pieces at once and you charged me $0.04 tax. What's going on?"

9.3 **Practice**
For use after Lesson 9.3

Write an equation for the function. Then complete the table.

1. The output is half of the input.

Input, x	0	2	4	6
Output, y				

2. The output is 5 less than the input.

Input, x	5	7	9	11
Output, y				

Write an equation for the function shown by the table.

3.

Input, x	1	2	3	4
Output, y	7	8	9	10

4.

Input, x	0	3	5	9
Output, y	0	6	10	18

Complete the table.

5. For each output, multiply the input by 8, then add 3.

Input, x	1	5		
Output, y	11	43	59	83

6. For each output, divide the input by 4, then subtract 1.

Input, x	4	8		
Output, y	0	1	2	3

7. You take a class to learn sign language. It costs $8 for each class you attend. Complete the input-output table. Write a function rule in which x is the input and y is the output.

Class, x	1	2	3	4
Cost, y				

Name_____ Date _____

Essential Question How can you use a graph to describe a function?

1 ACTIVITY: Interpreting a Graph

Work with a partner. Use a graph to test the truth of each statement. If the statement is true, write an equation that shows how to get one measurement from the other measurement.

a. "You can find the horsepower of a race car engine if you know its volume in cubic inches."

b. "You can find the volume of a race car engine in cubic centimeters if you know its volume in cubic inches."

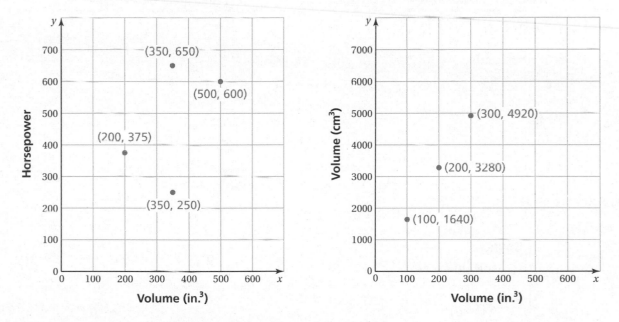

2 ACTIVITY: Interpreting a Graph

Work with a partner. The table shows the average speeds of the winners of the Daytona 500. Graph the data on the next page. Does the graph allow you to predict future winning speeds? Explain why or why not.

Year	2000	2001	2002	2003	2004	2005	2006	2007	2008
Speed (mi/h)	156	162	143	134	156	135	143	149	153

9.4 **Graphs** (continued)

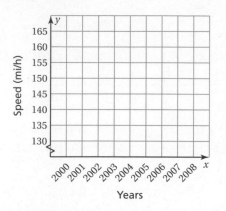

Years

ACTIVITY: Conducting an Experiment

Work with a partner.

Collect Materials:

- Metal washer, string (at least 15 in. long), stopwatch

Perform the Experiment:

- Tie one end of the string securely around the washer.

- Hold the string 6 inches from the washer. Swing the washer and measure the time it takes to swing back and forth 10 times.

- Record your result in a table.

String Length (in.)	6	7	8	9	10	11	12
Time (sec)							

- Repeat the experiment when holding the string at lengths of 7 in., 8 in., 9 in., 10 in., 11 in., and 12 in.

Analyze the Results:

- Make a graph of your data.

- Describe the graph.

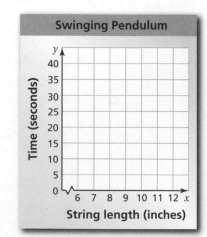

9.4 Graphs (continued)

Use Your Results to Predict:

- Use your graph to predict how long it will take a 14-inch pendulum to swing 10 times.

Test Your Prediction:

- Hold the string 14 inches from the washer and repeat the experiment. How close was your prediction?

What Is Your Answer?

4. **IN YOUR OWN WORDS** How can you use a graph to describe a function? Find a graph in a magazine, in a newspaper, or on the Internet that allows you to predict the future.

"I graphed our profits."

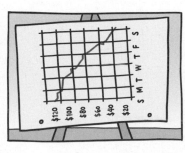

"And I am happy to say that they are going up every day!"

Name _____ Date _____

Graph the data.

1.

Input, x	2	4	6	8
Output, y	0	2	4	6

2.

Input, x	1	2	3	4
Output, y	7	10	13	16

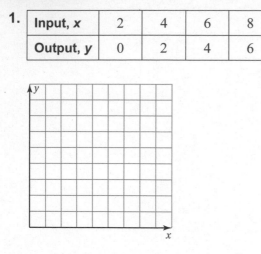

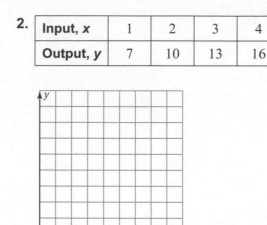

Graph the function.

3. $y = \dfrac{x}{10}$

4. $y = \dfrac{1}{2}x + 3$

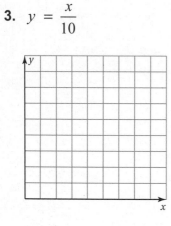

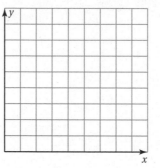

5. While on vacation, you buy key chains for your friends. Each key chain costs $3. You have a coupon for $2 off your entire purchase. The function $c = 3k - 2$ relates the number of key chains k you buy and your cost c. Graph the function.

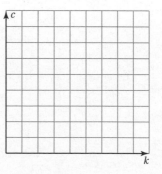

Name_____ Date_____

9.5 Analyzing Graphs
For use with Activity 9.5

Essential Question How can you analyze a function from its graph?

1 ACTIVITY: Analyzing Graphs

Work with a partner. Complete the table for the given situation. Then make a graph of the data. Write an equation for the function. Describe the characteristics of the graph.

a. Find the area of a square with side length s.

Side, s	1	2	3	4
Area, A				

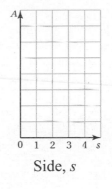

Side, s

b. Find the amount earned for working h hours at $3 per hour.

Hour, h	1	2	3	4
Amount, A				

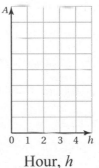

Hour, h

c. You start with $20 in a savings account. Find the amount left in the account when you withdraw $2 each day d.

Day, d	1	2	3	4
Amount, A				

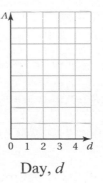

Day, d

9.5 Analyzing Graphs (continued)

d. You start with $10 in a savings account. Find the amount in the account when you deposit $2 each day d.

Day, d	1	2	3	4
Amount, A				

Day, d

---

2 ACTIVITY: Conducting an Experiment

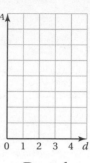

Work with a partner.

Collect Materials:

- A board at least 8 feet long
- Five books of the same thickness
- Toy car
- Stopwatch

Perform the Experiment:

- Place one book underneath one end of the board.
- Put the car at the top of the ramp. Measure the time (in seconds) it takes the car to roll down the ramp.
- Record your result in a table.

Number of Books	1	2	3	4
Time (seconds)				

- Repeat the experiment with two, three, and four books.

9.5 **Analyzing Graphs** (continued)

Analyze the Results:

- Make a graph of your data.

- Does the graph have the characteristics of any of the graphs in Activity 1? Explain.

Use Your Results to Predict:

- Use your graph to predict how long it will take the car to roll down the ramp when five books are placed under the board.

Test Your Prediction:

- Repeat the experiment with five books. How close was your prediction?

What Is Your Answer?

3. **IN YOUR OWN WORDS** How can you analyze a function from its graph? Give a real-life example of how a graph can help you make a decision.

9.5 **Practice**
For use after Lesson 9.5

Does the graph represent a linear function? Explain.

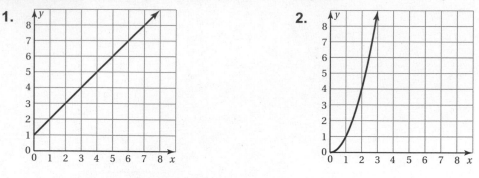

1.

2.

Does the input-output table represent a linear function? Explain.

3.

Input, x	0	3	5	9
Output, y	0	6	10	18

4.

Input, x	1	4	9	16
Output, y	1	2	3	4

Graph each linear function. Which graph is steeper? Explain.

5. $y = 3x$ and $y = \frac{1}{3}x$

6. $y = \frac{3}{8}x$ and $y = \frac{5}{8}x$

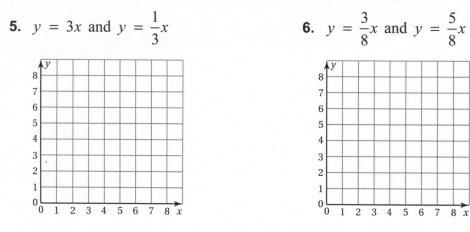

7. The graphs show the number of shirts and pants sales during a week. Which item has more sales in a day? How much more? Explain.

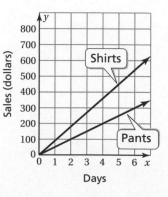

Name_____ Date_____

Additional Topics **Fair Game Review**

Use a number line to order the numbers from least to greatest.

1. 3, 6, 5, 1, 0

2. 2, 8, 6, 7, 4

3. 14, 5, 12, 13, 6

4. 32, 38, 40, 35, 37

5. 10, 25, 15, 30, 5

6. 30, 62, 55, 47, 19

7. 80, 87, 86, 88, 82, 92

8. 90, 102, 98, 87, 105, 94

9. The numbers of seconds it took 5 turtles to complete a turtle race are 115, 43, 180, 20, and 85. Use a number line to order the times from least to greatest.

Additional Topics **Fair Game Review** (continued)

Use the graph to answer the question.

10. Which point is located at $(2, 5)$?

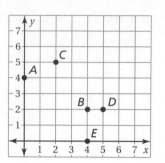

11. Which point is located at $(5, 2)$?

12. Which point is located at $(0, 4)$?

13. Which point is located at $(4, 0)$?

Find the perimeter of the triangle or rectangle.

14.

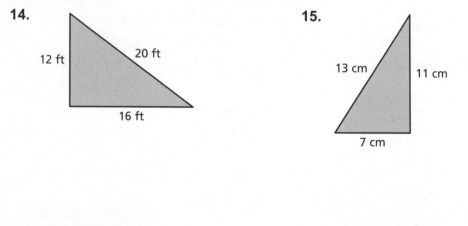

12 ft   20 ft

16 ft

15.

13 cm   11 cm

7 cm

16.

5 m

8 m

17.

14 in.

14 in.

Topic 1 Practice
For use after Topic 1

Write a positive or negative integer that represents the situation.

1. You withdraw $42 from an account.

2. An airplane climbs 37,500 feet.

3. You lose 56 points in a video game.

4. You receive 5 bonus points in class.

Graph the integer and its opposite.

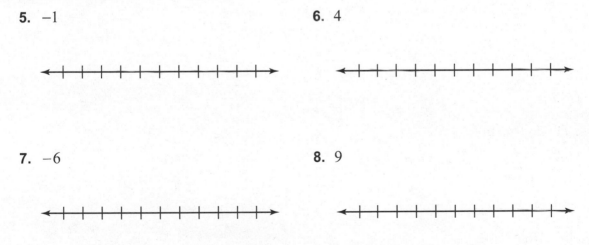

5. −1

6. 4

7. −6

8. 9

Name _____ Date _____

Identify the integer represented by the point on the vertical number line.

9. *A*

10. *B*

11. *C*

12. *D*

13. You earn $50 for babysitting. Two days later, you spend $20 on a necklace. Write each amount as an integer. Explain the meaning of zero in this context.

14. The world record for scuba diving is 318 meters below sea level. Write this as an integer. Explain the meaning of zero in this context.

15. Use the information below.

    • Low tide is 1 foot below the mean water level.

    • High tide is 5 feet higher than low tide.

    Write an integer that represents the mean water level relative to high tide.

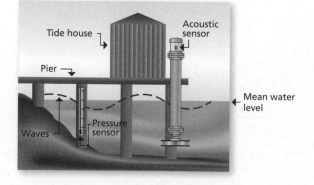

Name_____ Date_____

Topic 2 **Practice**
For use after Topic 2

Complete the statement using < or >.

1. 3 _____ 0

2. 6 _____ −6

3. −8 _____ −7

4. −1 _____ 4

5. 3.7 _____ −3.2

6. −1.6 _____ 0.3

7. −0.9 _____ −1.1

8. −10.4 _____ −10.04

9. $-\dfrac{2}{3}$ _____ $\dfrac{1}{4}$

10. $-\dfrac{1}{6}$ _____ $-\dfrac{1}{2}$

11. $-1\dfrac{3}{4}$ _____ $-1\dfrac{6}{7}$

12. $-2\dfrac{2}{3}$ _____ $-2\dfrac{1}{2}$

Order the numbers from least to greatest.

13. −2, 0, −4, 2, 3

14. −6.3, 4.2, 7.7, −3.9, 3.4

15. $1\dfrac{4}{5}, \dfrac{1}{2}, -3\dfrac{7}{8}, -\dfrac{7}{9}, -\dfrac{3}{5}$

16. $-3, 0.6, \dfrac{1}{4}, 0, -1\dfrac{2}{3}$

Topic 2 **Practice** (continued)

17. An archaeologist discovers two artifacts.
Compare the positions of the artifacts.

18. The table shows the highest and lowest
elevations for five states.

    a. Order the states by their highest
       elevations, from least to greatest.
       Which state has the highest elevation?

State	Highest Elevation (ft)	Lowest Elevation (ft)
Arkansas	2753	55
California	14,494	−282
Florida	345	0
Louisiana	535	−8
Tennessee	6643	178

    b. Order the states by their lowest
       elevations, from least to greatest.
       Which state has the lowest elevation?

Topic 3

Practice
For use after Topic 3

Find the absolute value.

1. $|-3|$

2. $|23|$

3. $|11|$

4. $|-9|$

5. $|-0.5|$

6. $|2.3|$

7. $\left|\dfrac{1}{4}\right|$

8. $\left|-3\dfrac{2}{3}\right|$

Complete the statement using <, >, or =.

9. 6 _____ $|-8|$

10. $|-3|$ _____ 3

11. $|-10|$ _____ $|-9|$

12. $|-7|$ _____ $|-5|$

13. $|-3.6|$ _____ $|5.1|$

14. $-\dfrac{5}{2}$ _____ $\left|3\dfrac{3}{4}\right|$

Name _____ Date _____

Tell which bank account balance is farther from $0.

15. Account A: −$10
    Account B: $11

16. Account A: −$36
    Account B: −$33

17. Account A: $100
    Account B: $50

18. Account A: $68
    Account B: −$87

19. The elevations of four fish are shown.

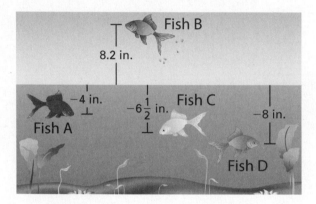

a. Which fish is the deepest? Explain.

b. Which fish is closest to sea level? Explain.

Topic 4 **Practice**
For use after Topic 4

Plot the ordered pair in the coordinate plane. Describe the location of the point.

1. $L(5, 8)$

2. $M(-7, 0)$

3. $N(-5, -8)$

4. $P(0, 9)$

5. $Q(-4.5, 1.5)$

6. $R\left(4\frac{1}{2}, 6\frac{1}{2}\right)$

7. The points $A(-1, -2)$, $B(-1, 1)$, $C(2, 1)$, and $D(2, -2)$ are vertices of a polygon.

   a. Graph the polygon in the coordinate plane.

   b. Find the perimeter of the polygon.

   c. Find the area of the polygon.

Topic 4 Practice (continued)

Match the description with the point that it represents.

8. A reflection of point A in the x-axis   **A.** $(-2, -3)$

9. A reflection of point B in the y-axis   **B.** $(3, 4)$

10. A reflection of point C in the y-axis, then the x-axis   **C.** $(-2, -2)$

Use the map of the city to find the distance between the given locations. Each unit represents 1 mile.

11. City Hall and School

12. Subway and Post Office

13. Museum and Post Office

14. Subway and City Hall

15. Park and Subway

16. Theater and Post Office

Glossary

This student friendly glossary is designed to be a reference for key vocabulary, properties, and mathematical terms. Several of the entries include a short example to aid your understanding of important concepts.

Also available at BigIdeasMath.com:

- multi-language glossary
- vocabulary flash cards

absolute value	**addend**
The distance between a number and 0 on a number line. The absolute value of a number a is written as $\lvert a \rvert$. $$\lvert -5 \rvert = 5$$ $$\lvert 5 \rvert = 5$$	A number to be added to another number. 2 or 3 in the sum $2 + 3$.
Addition Property of Equality	**Addition Property of Inequality**
If you add the same number to each side of an equation, the two sides remain equal. $$\begin{array}{rr} x - 4 = & 5 \\ +\,4 \quad & +\,4 \\ \hline x = & 9 \end{array}$$	If you add the same number to each side of an inequality, the inequality remains true. $$\begin{array}{rr} x - 4 > & 5 \\ +\,4 \quad & +\,4 \\ \hline x > & 9 \end{array}$$
Addition Property of Zero	**algebraic expression**
The sum of any number and 0 is that number. $$5 + 0 = 5$$	An expression that contains numbers, operations, and one or more variables. $$8 + x,\; 6 \times a - b$$

angle

A figure formed by two rays with the same endpoint.

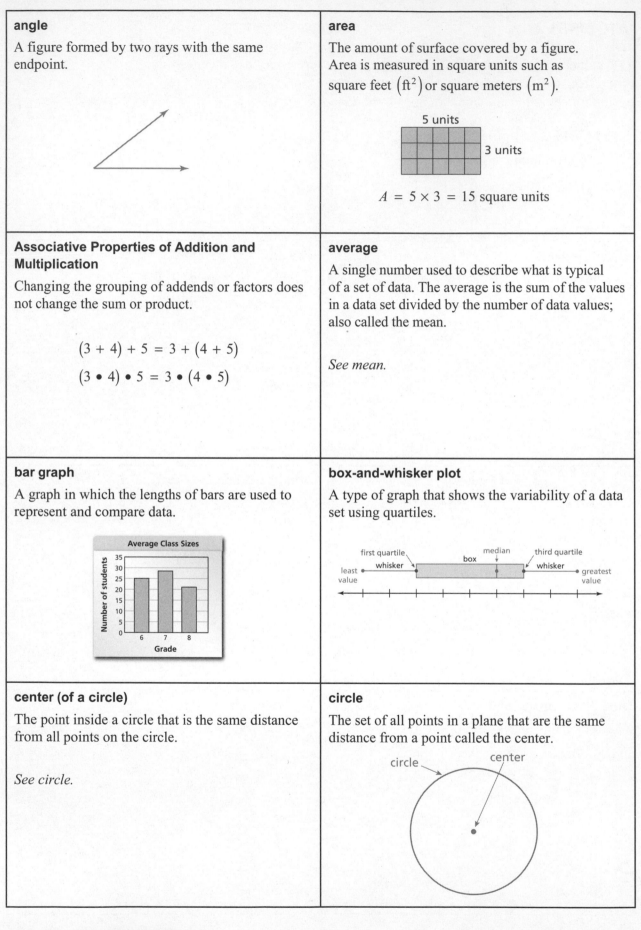

area

The amount of surface covered by a figure. Area is measured in square units such as square feet (ft^2) or square meters (m^2).

5 units

3 units

$A = 5 \times 3 = 15$ square units

Associative Properties of Addition and Multiplication

Changing the grouping of addends or factors does not change the sum or product.

$$(3 + 4) + 5 = 3 + (4 + 5)$$
$$(3 \bullet 4) \bullet 5 = 3 \bullet (4 \bullet 5)$$

average

A single number used to describe what is typical of a set of data. The average is the sum of the values in a data set divided by the number of data values; also called the mean.

See mean.

bar graph

A graph in which the lengths of bars are used to represent and compare data.

Average Class Sizes

Number of students

Grade

box-and-whisker plot

A type of graph that shows the variability of a data set using quartiles.

first quartile   median   third quartile
least   whisker   box   whisker   greatest
value   value

center (of a circle)

The point inside a circle that is the same distance from all points on the circle.

See circle.

circle

The set of all points in a plane that are the same distance from a point called the center.

circle   center

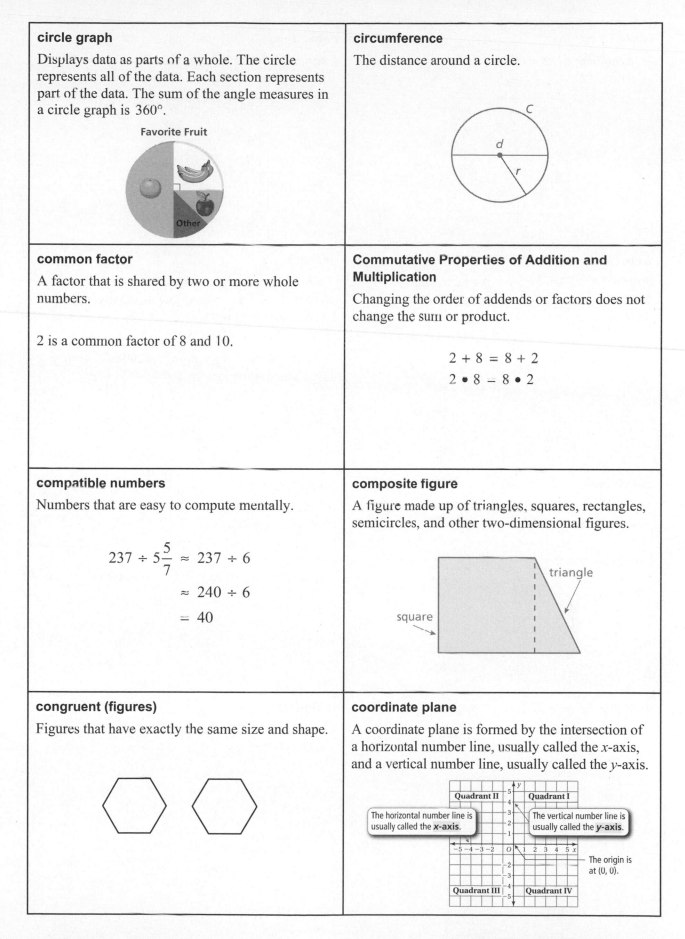

circle graph

Displays data as parts of a whole. The circle represents all of the data. Each section represents part of the data. The sum of the angle measures in a circle graph is 360°.

Favorite Fruit

Other

circumference

The distance around a circle.

C

d

r

common factor

A factor that is shared by two or more whole numbers.

2 is a common factor of 8 and 10.

Commutative Properties of Addition and Multiplication

Changing the order of addends or factors does not change the sum or product.

$$2 + 8 = 8 + 2$$
$$2 \bullet 8 = 8 \bullet 2$$

compatible numbers

Numbers that are easy to compute mentally.

$$237 \div 5\frac{5}{7} \approx 237 \div 6$$
$$\approx 240 \div 6$$
$$= 40$$

composite figure

A figure made up of triangles, squares, rectangles, semicircles, and other two-dimensional figures.

triangle

square

congruent (figures)

Figures that have exactly the same size and shape.

coordinate plane

A coordinate plane is formed by the intersection of a horizontal number line, usually called the x-axis, and a vertical number line, usually called the y-axis.

Quadrant II   Quadrant I

The horizontal number line is usually called the **x-axis**.

The vertical number line is usually called the **y-axis**.

The origin is at (0, 0).

Quadrant III   Quadrant IV

cube	**cubic units**
A rectangular prism with 6 congruent square faces.	The units volume is measured in. $$\text{cubic feet } (\text{ft}^3), \text{ cubic meters } (\text{m}^3)$$
data	**decimal**
Information, often given in the form of numbers or facts.	A number that is written using the base-ten place value system. Each place value is ten times the place value to the right. The decimal 2.15 represents 2 ones plus 1 tenth plus 5 hundredths, or two and fifteen hundredths.
denominator	**diagonal**
The number below the fraction bar in a fraction. In the fraction $\dfrac{2}{5}$, the denominator is 5.	A line segment that connects two non-adjacent vertices of a polygon. diagonal of a rectangle
diameter (of a circle)	**difference**
The distance across a circle through the center. *See circumference.*	The result when one number is subtracted from another number. The difference of 4 and 3 is $4 - 3$, or 1.

Distributive Property	**dividend**
To multiply a sum or difference by a number, multiply each number in the sum or difference by the number outside the parentheses. Then evaluate. $$3(2 + 9) = 3(2) + 3(9)$$ $$3(2 - 9) = 3(2) - 3(9)$$	The number to be divided in a division problem. In $25 \div 5$, the dividend is 25.
divisible	**Division Property of Equality**
A number is divisible by another number if the other number is a factor of the first number. 30 is divisible by 5, because 5 is a factor of 30.	If you divide each side of an equation by the same nonzero number, the two sides remain equal. $$4x = 32$$ $$\frac{4x}{4} = \frac{32}{4}$$ $$x = 8$$
Division Property of Inequality	**divisor**
If you divide each side of an inequality by the same positive number, the inequality remains true. $$4x < 8$$ $$\frac{4x}{4} < \frac{8}{4}$$ $$x < 2$$	The number you are dividing by in a division problem. In $40 \div 5$, the divisor is 5.
double bar graph	**equation**
A bar graph that shows two sets of data on the same graph. Average Test Scores	A mathematical sentence that uses an equal sign, =, to show that two expressions are equal. $$4x = 16, \ a + 7 = 21$$

equivalent expressions	**equivalent fractions**
Expressions with the same value.	Fractions that represent the same number.
$7 + 4,\ 4 + 7$	$\dfrac{2}{4}$ and $\dfrac{9}{18}$ are equivalent fractions that both represent $\dfrac{1}{2}$.

equivalent ratios	**estimate**
Two ratios that describe the same relationship.	noun: An approximate solution to a problem.
$\dfrac{2}{3} = \dfrac{4}{6}$	2π is about 6.28.
	verb: To find an approximate solution to a problem.
	You can estimate the sum of $98 + 53$ as $100 + 50$, or 150.

evaluate (an algebraic expression)	**exponent**
Substitute a number for each variable in an algebraic expression. Then use the order of operations to find the value of the numerical expression.	The exponent of a power is the number of times the factor is repeated.
Evaluate $3x + 5$ when $x = 6$.	The exponent of the power 2^4 is 4.
$\begin{aligned} 3x + 5 &= 3(6) + 5 \\ &= 18 + 5 \\ &= 23 \end{aligned}$	

expression	**factor**
A mathematical phrase containing numbers, operations, and/or variables.	When whole numbers other than zero are multiplied together, each number is a factor of the product.
See numerical expression or algebraic expression.	$2 \times 3 \times 4 = 24$, so 2, 3, and 4 are factors of 24.

formula	**fraction**
An equation that shows how one variable is related to one or more other variables. $A = \ell w$ is the formula for the area of a rectangle.	A number in the form $\dfrac{a}{b}$, where $b \neq 0$. $$\dfrac{1}{2}, \dfrac{5}{9}$$

function	**function rule**
A relationship that pairs each input with exactly one output. The ordered pairs $(0, 1)$, $(1, 2)$, $(2, 4)$, and $(3, 6)$ represent a function. **Ordered Pairs** $(0, 1)$ $(1, 2)$ $(2, 4)$ $(3, 6)$ Input → Output 0 → 1 1 → 2 2 → 4 3 → 6	An equation that describes the relationship between inputs and outputs. The function rule "the output is three less than the input" is represented by the equation $y = x - 3$.

graph (of a function)	**graph of an inequality**
A representation of all the points that are solutions of a function rule. The graph of $y = x + 2$ is shown.	A graph that shows all of the solutions of an inequality on a number line. $$x > 2$$

greatest common factor (GCF)	**histogram**
The largest of the common factors of two or more nonzero whole numbers. The common factors of 12 and 20 are 1, 2, and 4. So the GCF of 12 and 20 is 4.	A bar graph that shows the frequency of data values in intervals of the same size. The height of a bar represents the frequency of the values in the interval. There are no spaces between bars.

improper fraction

A fraction in which the numerator is greater than or equal to the denominator.

$$\frac{5}{4}, \frac{9}{9}$$

inductive

Making conclusions from several known cases.

inequality

A mathematical sentence that compares expressions. It contains the symbols $<$, $>$, $\leq$, or $\geq$.

$$x - 4 < 14, \ x + 5 \geq 67$$

input

A number on which a function operates.

See function.

input-output table

A table that lists the output of a function for each input.

Input, x	Output, y
1	3
2	4
3	5
4	6

integers

The set of whole numbers and their opposites.

$$..., -5, -4, -3, -2, -1, 0, 1, 2, 3, 4, 5, ...$$

interquartile range

The range of the middle half of a data set. The interquartile range is the difference of the third quartile and the first quartile.

See quartiles.

inverse operations

Operations that "undo" each other, such as addition and subtraction or multiplication and division.

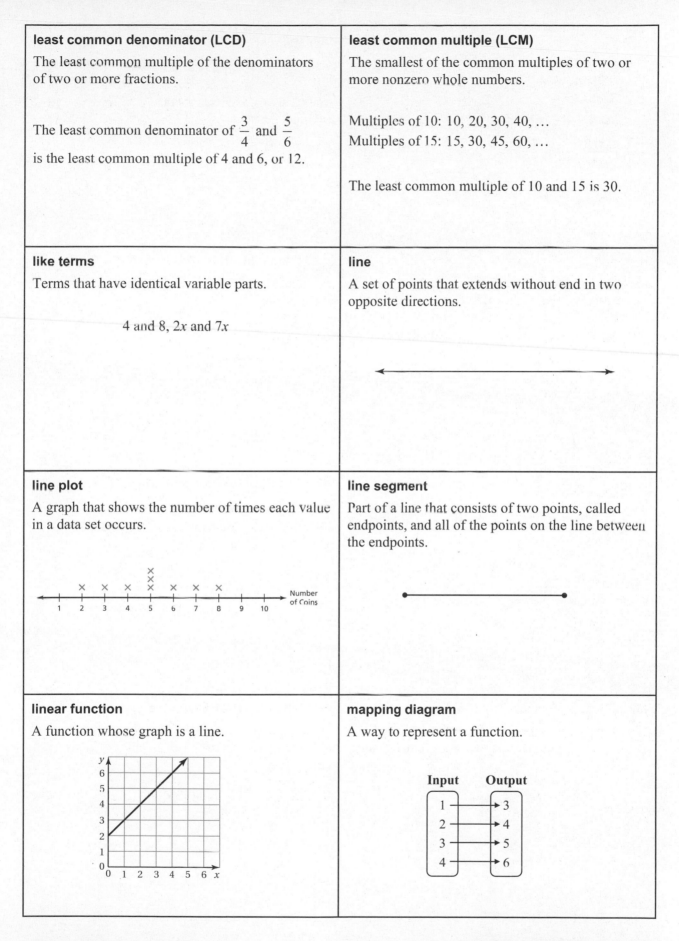

least common denominator (LCD)

The least common multiple of the denominators of two or more fractions.

The least common denominator of $\frac{3}{4}$ and $\frac{5}{6}$ is the least common multiple of 4 and 6, or 12.

least common multiple (LCM)

The smallest of the common multiples of two or more nonzero whole numbers.

Multiples of 10: 10, 20, 30, 40, …
Multiples of 15: 15, 30, 45, 60, …

The least common multiple of 10 and 15 is 30.

like terms

Terms that have identical variable parts.

4 and 8, $2x$ and $7x$

line

A set of points that extends without end in two opposite directions.

line plot

A graph that shows the number of times each value in a data set occurs.

line segment

Part of a line that consists of two points, called endpoints, and all of the points on the line between the endpoints.

linear function

A function whose graph is a line.

mapping diagram

A way to represent a function.

Input	Output
1	3
2	4
3	5
4	6

mean

The sum of the values in a data set divided by the number of data values.

The mean of the values 7, 4, 8, and 9 is

$$\frac{7 + 4 + 8 + 9}{4} = \frac{28}{4} = 7.$$

measure of central tendency

A measure that represents the center of a data set.

The mean, median, and mode are all measures of central tendency.

median

For a data set with an odd number of ordered values, the median is the middle data value. For a data set with an even number of ordered values, the median is the mean of the two middle values.

The median of the data set 24, 25, 29, 33, 38 is 29 because 29 is the middle value.

mixed number

A number that has a whole number part and a fraction part.

$$3\frac{1}{2}, 6\frac{2}{3}$$

mode

The data value or values that occur most often. Data can have one mode, more than one mode, or no mode.

The modes of the data set 3, 4, 4, 7, 7, 9, 12 are 4 and 7 because they occur most often.

Multiplication Properties of Zero and One

The product of any number and 0 is 0.
The product of any number and 1 is that number.

$$5 \bullet 0 = 0$$
$$6 \bullet 1 = 6$$

Multiplication Property of Equality

If you multiply each side of an equation by the same nonzero number, the two sides remain equal.

$$\frac{x}{4} = 2$$

$$\frac{x}{4} \bullet 4 = 2 \bullet 4$$

$$x = 8$$

Multiplication Property of Inequality

If you multiply each side of an inequality by the same positive number, the inequality remains true.

$$\frac{x}{4} < 2$$

$$\frac{x}{4} \bullet 4 < 2 \bullet 4$$

$$x < 8$$

negative integers Integers that are less than zero. $$-1, -2, -3, -4, -5, \ldots$$	**negative number** A number less than 0. $$-0.25, -10, -500$$
net A two-dimensional representation of a solid. 	**number line** A line whose points are associated with numbers that increase from left to right.
numerator The number above the fraction bar in a fraction. In the fraction $\dfrac{2}{5}$, the numerator is 2.	**numerical expression** An expression that contains only numbers and operations. $$12 + 6, \, 18 + 3 \times 4$$
opposites Two numbers that are the same distance from 0, but on opposite sides of 0. -3 and 3 are opposites.	**order of operations** The order in which to perform operations when evaluating expressions with more than one operation. To evaluate $5 + 2 \times 3$, you perform the multiplication before the addition.

ordered pair

A pair of numbers (x, y) used to locate a point in a coordinate plane. The first number is the x-coordinate, and the second number is the y-coordinate.

The x-coordinate of the point $(-2, 1)$ is -2, and the y-coordinate is 1.

origin

The point, represented by the ordered pair $(0, 0)$, where the x-axis and the y-axis meet in a coordinate plane.

See coordinate plane.

outlier

A data value that is much greater or much less than the other values.

In the data set 23, 42, 33, 117, 36, and 40, the outlier is 117.

output

A number produced by evaluating a function using a given input.

See function.

overestimate

An estimate that is greater than the exact answer.

$$16\frac{1}{4} \times 4\frac{2}{5} \approx 17 \times 5$$
$$= 85$$

parallel (lines)

Two lines in the same plane that do not intersect.

Indicates lines p and q are parallel.

parallelogram

A quadrilateral with two pairs of parallel sides.

percent

The number of parts per one hundred.

$$37\% = 37 \text{ out of } 100 = \frac{37}{100}$$

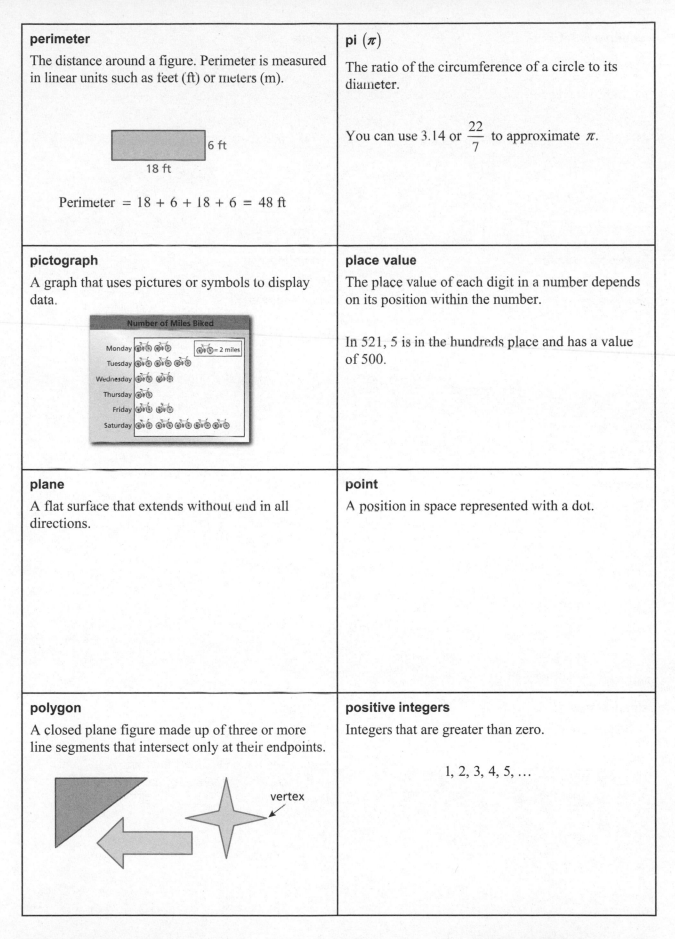

perimeter

The distance around a figure. Perimeter is measured in linear units such as feet (ft) or meters (m).

6 ft
18 ft

Perimeter = 18 + 6 + 18 + 6 = 48 ft

pi (π)

The ratio of the circumference of a circle to its diameter.

You can use 3.14 or $\frac{22}{7}$ to approximate π.

pictograph

A graph that uses pictures or symbols to display data.

Number of Miles Biked

Monday
Tuesday
Wednesday
Thursday
Friday
Saturday

= 2 miles

place value

The place value of each digit in a number depends on its position within the number.

In 521, 5 is in the hundreds place and has a value of 500.

plane

A flat surface that extends without end in all directions.

point

A position in space represented with a dot.

polygon

A closed plane figure made up of three or more line segments that intersect only at their endpoints.

vertex

positive integers

Integers that are greater than zero.

1, 2, 3, 4, 5, …

positive number	power
A number greater than 0. 0.5, 2, 100	A product formed from repeated multiplication by the same number or expression. A power consists of a base and an exponent. 2^4 is a power with base 2 and exponent 4.
prime factorization	**prime number**
A whole number written as the product of prime numbers. $60 = 2 \times 2 \times 3 \times 5$	A whole number greater than 1 whose only factors are 1 and itself. 2, 3, 5, 7, 11, 13, 17, 19, 23, 29, 31, ...
product	**quadrants**
The result when two or more numbers are multiplied. The product of 4 and 3 is 4×3, or 12.	The four regions created by the intersection of the *x*-axis and the *y*-axis in a coordinate plane. *See coordinate plane.*
quadrilateral	**quartiles**
A polygon with four sides.	Used to divide a data set into four equal parts. The median (second quartile) divides the data set into two halves. The median of the lower half is the first quartile. The median of the upper half is the third quartile. *See box-and-whisker plot.*

quotient The result of a division. The quotient of 10 and 5 is 10 ÷ 5, or 2.	**radius (of a circle)** The distance from the center of a circle to any point on the circle. *See circumference.*
range (of a data set) The difference between the greatest value and the least value of a data set. The range describes how spread out the data are. The range of the data set 12, 16, 18, 22, 27, 35 is $35 - 12 = 23$.	**rate** A ratio of two quantities with different units. You read 3 books every 2 weeks.
ratio A comparison of two quantities using division. The ratio of a to b (where $b \neq 0$) can be written as a to b, $a : b$, or $\dfrac{a}{b}$. $$4 \text{ to } 1, \ 4 : 1, \text{ or } \frac{4}{1}$$	**ray** A part of a line that has one endpoint and extends without end in one direction. •————————▶
reciprocals Two numbers whose product is 1. Because $\dfrac{4}{5} \times \dfrac{5}{4} = 1$, $\dfrac{4}{5}$ and $\dfrac{5}{4}$ are reciprocals.	**rectangle** A parallelogram with four right angles.

rectangular prism	**remainder**
A three-dimensional figure that has 6 rectangular sides.	If a divisor does not divide a dividend evenly, the remainder is the whole number left over after the division.
	$$\begin{array}{r} 4 \\ 7\overline{)30} \\ \underline{28} \\ 2 \end{array}$$ R 2 The remainder is 2.

repeating decimal	**round**
A decimal that repeats a pattern of one or more digits.	To approximate a number to a given place value.
$$0.555\ldots = 0.\overline{5}$$ $$1.727272\ldots = 1.\overline{72}$$	132 rounded to the nearest ten is 130.

semicircle	**simplest form of a fraction**
One half of a circle.	A fraction is in simplest form if its numerator and denominator have a greatest common factor (GCF) of 1.
	The simplest form of the fraction $\frac{10}{15}$ is $\frac{2}{3}$.

solution (of an equation)	**solution of an inequality**
A value that makes an equation true.	A value that makes an inequality true.
6 is the solution of the equation $x - 4 = 2$.	A solution of the inequality $x + 3 > 9$ is $x = 12$.

solution set

The set of all solutions of an inequality.

solve a formula

Find the value of one variable by substituting numbers for the other variables.

$$\ell = 6 \text{ in.}, \ w = 10 \text{ in.}$$
$$P = 2\ell + 2w$$
$$= 2(6) + 2(10)$$
$$= 32 \text{ in.}$$

square

A parallelogram with four right angles and four sides of equal length.

square pyramid

A three-dimensional figure that has one square face and four identical triangular faces.

square units

The units surface area and area are measured in.

square inches $\left(\text{in.}^2\right)$, square meters $\left(\text{m}^2\right)$

Subtraction Property of Equality

If you subtract the same number from each side of an equation, the two sides remain equal.

$$
\begin{array}{rr}
x + 4 = & 5 \\
-4 & -4 \\
\hline
x = & 1
\end{array}
$$

Subtraction Property of Inequality

If you subtract the same number from each side of an inequality, the inequality remains true.

$$
\begin{array}{rr}
x + 4 > & 5 \\
-4 & -4 \\
\hline
x > & 1
\end{array}
$$

sum

The result when two or more numbers are added.

The sum of 4 and 3 is $4 + 3$, or 7.

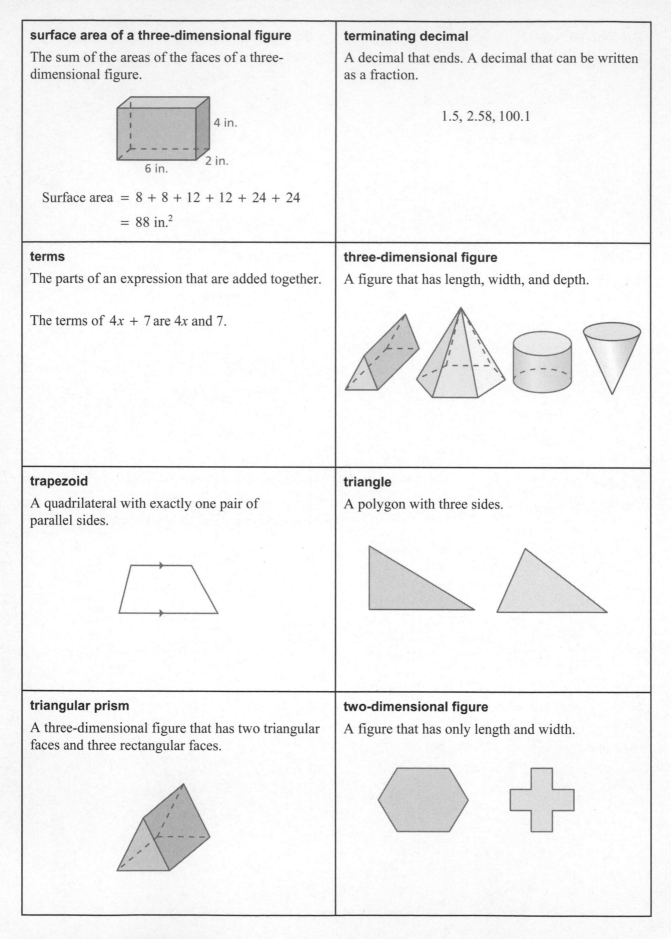

surface area of a three-dimensional figure

The sum of the areas of the faces of a three-dimensional figure.

4 in.

6 in. 2 in.

Surface area $= 8 + 8 + 12 + 12 + 24 + 24$
$= 88$ in.^{2}

terminating decimal

A decimal that ends. A decimal that can be written as a fraction.

1.5, 2.58, 100.1

terms

The parts of an expression that are added together.

The terms of $4x + 7$ are $4x$ and 7.

three-dimensional figure

A figure that has length, width, and depth.

trapezoid

A quadrilateral with exactly one pair of parallel sides.

triangle

A polygon with three sides.

triangular prism

A three-dimensional figure that has two triangular faces and three rectangular faces.

two-dimensional figure

A figure that has only length and width.

two-step equation An equation that contains two different operations. $$3x + 4 = 7,\ 2x - 5 = 13$$	**underestimate** An estimate that is less than the exact answer. $$35\frac{7}{8} \times 8\frac{1}{3} \approx 35 \times 8$$ $$= 280$$
unit cost A unit rate for cost per unit. The cost per bottle is $3.	**unit rate** A rate that compares a quantity to one unit of another quantity. The speed limit is 65 miles per hour.
variable A symbol, usually a letter, that represents one or more numbers. x is a variable in $2x + 1$.	**vertex of a polygon** A point at which two sides of a polygon meet. The plural of vertex is vertices. *See polygon.*
volume A measure of the amount of space that a three-dimensional figure occupies. Volume is measured in cubic units such as cubic feet $\left(\text{ft}^3\right)$ or cubic meters $\left(\text{m}^3\right)$. $$V = \ell wh = 12(3)(4) = 144\ \text{ft}^3$$	**whole numbers** The numbers $0, 1, 2, 3, 4, \ldots.$

x-axis	**x-coordinate**
The horizontal number line in a coordinate plane.	The first coordinate in an ordered pair, which indicates how many units to move to the left or right.
See coordinate plane.	In the ordered pair $(3, 5)$, the x-coordinate is 3.
y-axis	**y-coordinate**
The vertical number line in a coordinate plane.	The second coordinate in an ordered pair, which indicates how many units to move up or down.
See coordinate plane.	In the ordered pair $(3, 5)$, the y-coordinate is 5.

Photo Credits

134 ©iStockphoto.com/Jerry Koch, ©iStockphoto.com/
Chad Anderson; **164** Madeira Beach Fundamental
School; **167** ©iStockphoto.com/SUSARO;
168 *left* stevecadman; *center* David Shankbone;
right ©iStockphoto.com/ROBERTO ADRIAN;
183 NASA; **186** *top left and right, center left and
right, bottom left* Andreas Meyer; **187** Ozja;
208 ©iStockphoto.com/Michael Flippo

Cartoon Illustrations Tyler Stout

*Available at *BigIdeasMath.com.*

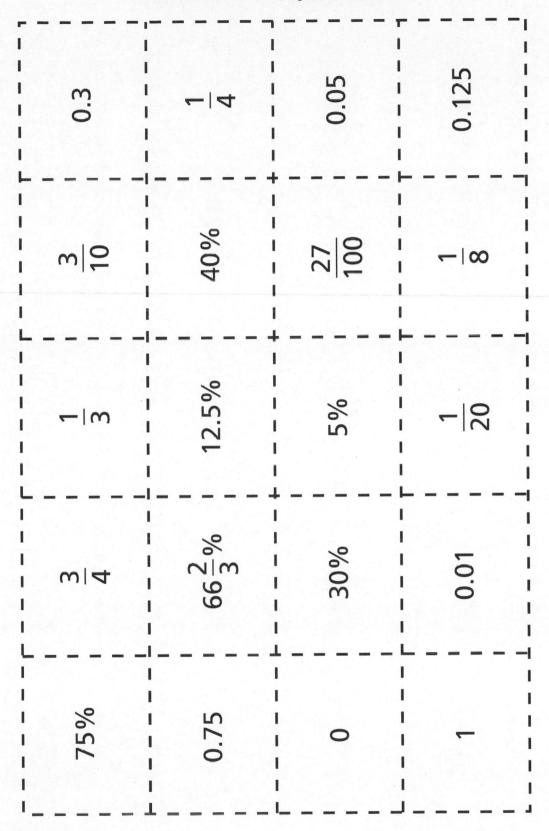

0.3	$\frac{1}{4}$	0.05	0.125
$\frac{3}{10}$	40%	$\frac{27}{100}$	$\frac{1}{8}$
$\frac{1}{3}$	12.5%	5%	$\frac{1}{20}$
$\frac{3}{4}$	$66\frac{2}{3}\%$	30%	0.01
75%	0.75	0	1

*Available at *BigIdeasMath.com.*

0.27	$\dfrac{2}{3}$	1%	0%
100%	$\dfrac{1}{100}$	27%	0.666...
0.25	0.04	0.333...	0.005
0.4	0.5%	$\dfrac{2}{5}$	$\dfrac{1}{200}$
25%	4%	$33\dfrac{1}{3}\%$	$\dfrac{1}{25}$

*Available at *BigIdeasMath.com.*

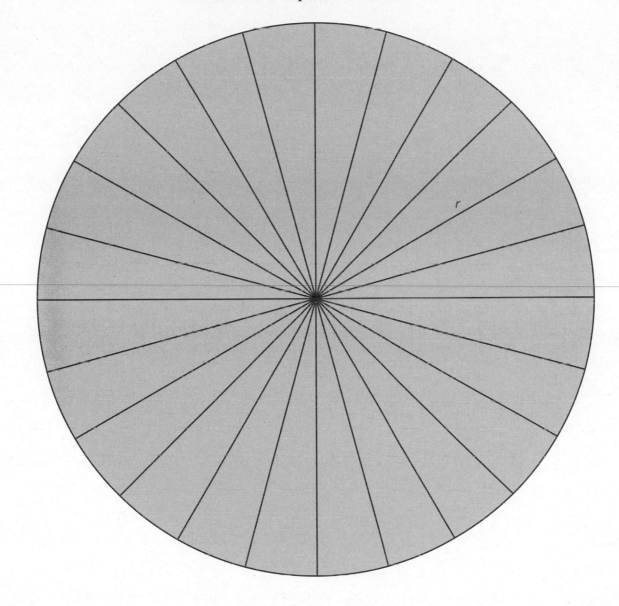

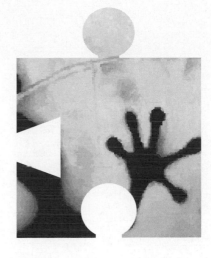

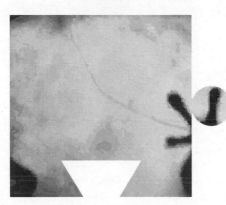

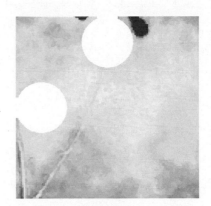

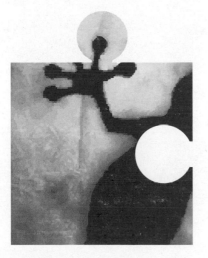

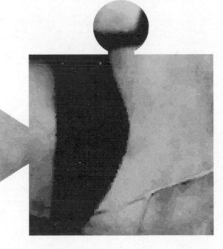

*Available at *BigIdeasMath.com*.

Pentagon – Chapter 8 Section 2*

Hexagon – Chapter 8 Section 2*

*Available at *BigIdeasMath.com*.

Base Ten Blocks*

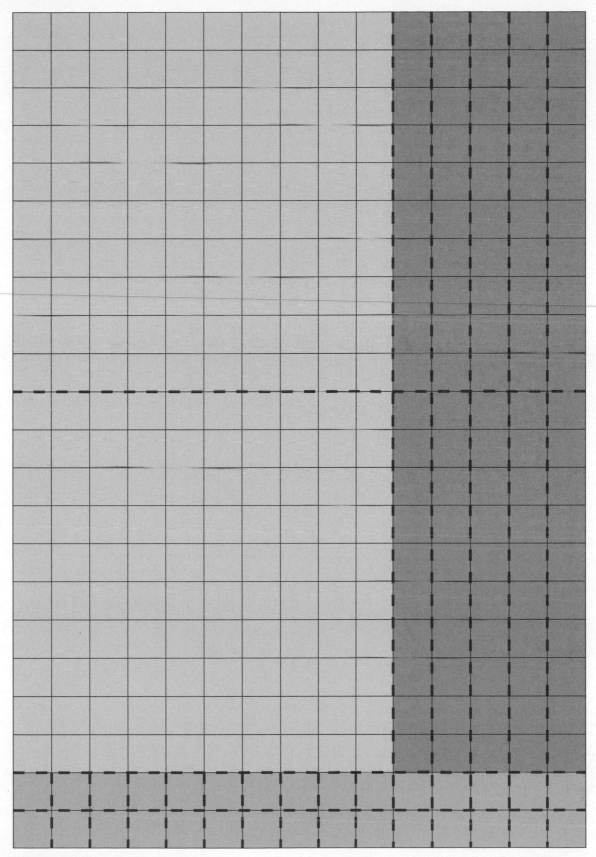

*Available at *BigIdeasMath.com*.

Base Ten Blocks*

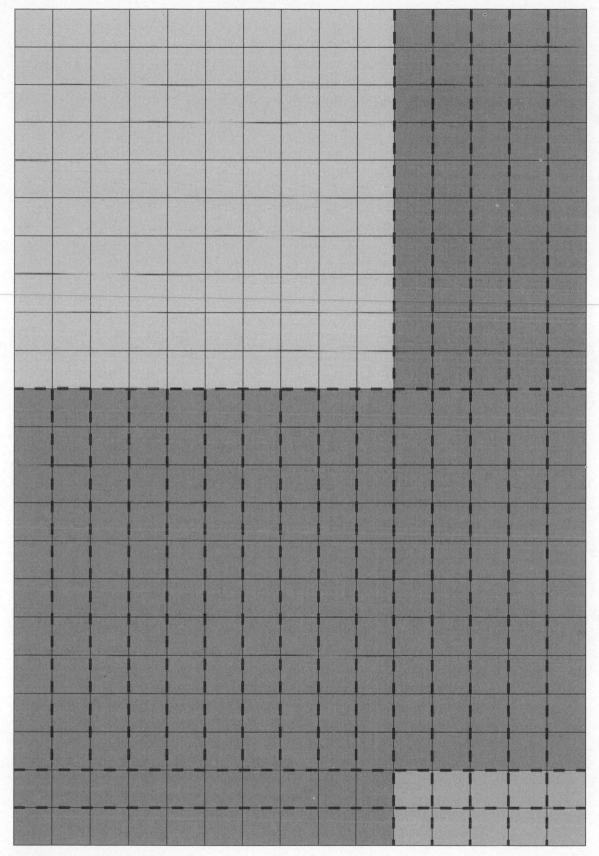

*Available at *BigIdeasMath.com*.